Ibukun Awosika

The

"Girl"

Entrepreneurs

Our Stories So Far...

Xulon
PRESS

DEDICATION

To the great I AM, the Almighty God. My El Shaddai, my King of kings. The One Who chose to make something out of nothing; Who chose an empty vessel and fill it with His Spirit.

How can I ever thank You for all that I have done and will ever do? I thank You LORD. If there is any glory, any wisdom for anything I have ever done in life, let it be to you O LORD. Because to You be all the glory, all the honour, all the praise and adoration, now and forever more. Amen.

ACKNOWLEDGMENTS

Through this book, I celebrate the three levels of authority in my life: my parents who taught me the true value of hard work, especially my mother for the boldness which I saw in her, for it takes boldness for a woman to leave her country as she did for my father at such a young age. My siblings and I are indebted to her for staying back against all odds to see that we become something. I wish she were here now to see the fruits of her labour. I thank my father for teaching us the value of hard work and for creating an environment where we were not made to think there was anything we could not do because we were girls.

Next, I celebrate my husband. Looking back many times through the path of deciding who to marry, I know how easy it is to have made a mistake. I celebrate you and thank you for all your support, for helping me to be who I am. I could not have made it this far without the assurance of your love.

And finally to my pastor, Pastor Taiwo, I say thank you for always being there. For the many moments when I knew you were praying for me, and for sharing in my many business burdens. I thank God for the many words of wisdom from the lips of Pastor Taiwo that guided me through many thorny decisions. To my dearest Pastor Bimbo, I celebrate your memory today and every day I will live. I can truly say on the pages of this book that I miss you. I know I had a fighter in you somewhere at the corner who was helping me to fight. I trust that, at the appropriate time, we will meet again, to part no more.

And to my dearest sons; Oludola, my first and my best. I couldn't have asked for a more gentle and fatherly young man to lead the pack. God made you complete. You are definitely going places.

To my fearless Olafusika, it is the fire inside you that will make many bow at your feet.

Acknowledgments

To my baby, Olamiposi, young and full of wisdom. I am certain you will be the best in your generation.

Thank you for all your sacrifices and your words of encouragement. In life and in death, wherever I may be, you can always be sure that no one could have loved you like your dearest mother.

CONTENTS

INTRODUCTION

I n the last few years as I have walked the path of building my business, I have consistently and continually encountered men and women, young and old, who have asked me questions on how to set up a business. Being a woman, how does one cope? How does one function in the marketplace? And how does one move from being a paid employee to an employer? And, even among those who are already in business, I am often asked such questions as how does one move from one stage to another in business?

I have come to realise that those who have had the privilege of building their own businesses from the scratch to a successful enterprise have a role to play in the enlightenment of others in the unsettling ground of business. I also realise that no matter the number of e-mails I reply through the TV programme I host, and no matter how many campuses or seminars I have been able to speak, I can only reach a few number of people at a time. But one thing I have learnt is that life itself is a great teacher. I therefore decided to seek out a few of my friends who have walked the path of entrepreneurship, and whose stories will help to inspire and encourage another person, young or old, male or female, who want to birth an enterprise to take the bold step.

As you read the stories of these women, you will find that they are all ordinary people like you who took unsure steps of faith; who had many moments of fear; who failed many times and yet got up again; who had many frustrating moments but yet refused to give up. And as they continued to push, the barriers that were hindering their paths gave way to them.

Their faith in their God is measured in their achievements. Their recognition and appreciation of the roles of their spouses and families in their businesses helped them to overcome every trying moment with a sense of adventure. And it makes the journey exciting, even when faced with many challenges.

Introduction

As you read this book, I want you to know that this story is not the end. For all these women are still work in progress; which is why even when they were humble enough to feel their story should not be shared, we still had to convince them to share it only so that you can have a reference point to get started.

YEWANDE ZACCHEAUS

1

Name:
YEWANDE ZACCHEAUS
(NEE AKINNOLA)

Name of Company:
EVENTFUL LIMITED

Post:
CEO

INDUSTRY:
EVENT PLANNING & MANAGEMENT

FAMILY BACKGROUND, CHILDHOOD, EDUCATION

I was born in Ibadan on April 17, 1961 to Chief & Mrs. Bayo Akinnola. I am the first born child in my family and was made to understand very early in life that I was in a position of leadership in the family.

I grew up accepting various responsibilities thrust upon me without any questions. I remember when I was 13, my parents decided that as a teenager I should no longer share a room with my siblings. I then moved to what had been the guest room. A room of my own! It was so significant at that time I was the de facto leader of the pack and I was responsible for influencing my siblings for good.

My family is extremely close knit and we have always shared and supported each others' dreams. My parents were both professionals who turned entrepreneurs in their early 40's, so for me this was a natural progression in the scheme of things. My father, Chief Bayo Akinnola, studied Education at the University of Ibadan and obtained a Post Graduate Diploma at Manchester

University. He started his life out as a teacher, and later veered into Human Resources Management at the Nigerian Tobacco Company before he was appointed Commissioner for Information and later for Home Affairs and Industries in the old Western State. It was after this stint in government that he set up his own manufacturing concern, Atobi Metal and Paper Industries Limited, which he is still running today at the grand old age of 73! As I write, he is presently on a business trip to India sourcing raw materials for the business.

My mother is a Chartered Secretary and Administrator who qualified at the Balham and Tooting College of Commerce, London, specializing in Taxation. She worked for several years at the Internal Revenue Board of the Western State, achieving the status of Chief Inspector of Taxes before retiring in January, 1979 to join my father in running the family business.

I set out this background in detail because I am convinced that the paths my parents chose, their example of integrity, professionalism, industry and enterprise clearly influenced the pattern of my own business life for good. We must be careful to ensure we set good examples for our children.

I attended the All Saints Church Primary School, Jericho Ibadan and the International School Ibadan for my primary and secondary education respectively. I was a good student and passed my WASC with a grade 1. I then proceeded to Clifton High School for Girls in Bristol England for my 'A' levels. Against my better judgement, but in fulfilment of my father's desire to have one of his children become a Dentist, (his mother died when he was very young from a tooth infection) I took A levels in Physics, Chemistry and Biology at Clifton. It was an unmitigated disaster.

I hated science, and no matter how hard I tried I could not fathom Physics and Chemistry. Needless to say I passed only Biology. I then persuaded my father to let me change to my preferred Art subjects, knowing that a re-take of Physics and Chemistry would be a waste of his money and my time! Fortunately he agreed and I went to Bedford Tutorial College, where I took 'A' level Sociology and Economics in one year and had excellent results.

I moved back to Nigeria to study Law at the University of Lagos from 1979 to 1982. I was a Merit Award winner and graduated with a Second Class Upper Division. I enjoyed my studies at UNILAG tremendously and was pleased to maintain the excellent academic grades at the Nigerian Law School. After Law School, I returned to England and took a Masters degree in Law at Jesus College, Cambridge University, where I also graduated with a Second Class Upper Division. I remember that out of about 8 of us Nigerians in the class, all, except one, made a Second Class Upper, a clear evidence of the fact that at that time the quality of education in Nigeria was clearly at par with that of the best universities in the world.

All the time I was growing up I always knew I would eventually run my own business some day. I wasn't quite clear what the business would be, but my vision was always of me sitting as a CEO in a fancy office directing people to do things!

My father has always been a very social person and an excellent host, and my mother a very detailed and organized woman. We were always hosting guests in our home and I grew up with a natural instinct for organizing parties, events, bossing my siblings around if the need arose, not realizing then that this experience would one day be honed into skills that would run a multi-million naira business.

Looking back now, I had a near idyllic childhood. Growing up in Ibadan was lovely. It was peaceful; our estate (Bodija) was children-friendly and serene. There were no walled fences, just hedges we could jump over at will to play with our friends. I remember clearly that one of the most exciting ways of having fun was rolling tyres down the road with other children. No PSP or Nintendo for us then. There was a real spirit of community we enjoyed that I fear no longer exists in our fractured society of today.

WORK EXPERIENCE
On my return from Cambridge, I began work in 1983 by observing my National Youth Corps at the Nigerian American Merchant Bank, Lagos. I worked as a legal officer in their legal department under the tutelage of Mrs. Aita Sogbetun, the Company Secretary/Legal Adviser of the bank at that time. She was an extremely meticulous and

organized person, and I acknowledge her contribution in shaping my career.

I worked at NAMBL for about 3 years. However, after a while I began to get restless about the routine of the work, and I decided that law practice appeared more interesting. So I resigned to join the firm of R.I. Kuku & Co., which was headed by Mrs. Rita Kuku, another consummate professional. Rita was somebody with a big vision and I learnt early from her that you project yourself and run your business based on where you want to go and not on where you are. Needless to say, I soon found out that the practice of law was not as it appeared in Perry Mason or LA Law! Cases took forever to be settled. In the two years I was in practice, I never saw one case through to the end. The entire justice system at that time, seemed cut out to frustrate one's aspirations. So I took another decision, out of practice and back to the corporate life for me!

I set out this background in some detail to encourage women to always think ahead and make career decisions based on what is best for them, what makes them happy and fulfilled, rather than just what is convenient. One of my father's favourite sayings to us when we were growing up was that we should not take the line of least resistance. I know it is not easy for everyone to take decisions that will significantly impact their lives in a way that may, or may not, turn out for good. But even so, life is for the living! We must occasionally take risks. We need to, as much as is within our power, dictate the course of our lives in the areas where we have a measure of control. Don't let life just happen to you. Think, take stock periodically and chart a course for your life based on your dreams and aspirations.

Fortunately for me, the time I took this decision was the time the new generation banks were being set up. I applied to several banks and received two offers. The first from Prime Bank, to be a legal officer under another senior colleague whom I admired and respected, Mrs. Kemi Ogunmefun or to be the Company Secretary and head of legal department of Ecobank Nigeria Plc where I knew no one but would have more responsibility. Prime's offer was more financially rewarding at that time, but I deliberately chose to go with

Ecobank's offer because of the position of responsibility and opportunities it offered. I have never had cause to regret that decision.

I worked in Ecobank for 13 years (1989 to 2002) serving in various capacities such as Company Secretary, Legal Adviser and Head of Private Banking. At various times during my time at Ecobank I was also responsible for the Corporate Affairs and Human Resources Department. I took full advantage of the opportunities for networking, career growth and travel that were available in Ecobank. This truly enhanced my professional life and I cannot begin to quantify the leverage that my experience and achievements in a first class bank has given me in my business today. I enjoyed a fulfilling career with the bank and learnt a lot about corporate governance, diplomacy and company politics from a seasoned and experienced Board of Directors. I acknowledge today the distinguished Nigerians who served as Chairman of the Board at different times and whom I worked with closely as Company Secretary, gaining invaluable experience. They are Chief P. C. Asiodu, Otunba Kunle Ojora, Mr. Dayo Sonuga and Chief A.O. Odimayo.

As was now usual with me, the restless spirit began to raise its head shortly after I resumed from maternity leave in 1999. I realised that when I got up in the morning the last place I wanted to go to was my office! I was BORED! I would attend Board and Management meetings and be totally out of it not connecting, not caring, just wanting out.

Ah! But those "golden handcuffs"... the fancy car, the air tickets and travel allowances, the fat monthly pay cheque whether you were productive or not, the perks, the prestige....all good... but I knew in my heart that it was over. I could have easily remained in the bank, delegating all my duties and collecting a hefty salary at the end of each month but I knew I couldn't live a lie and I had to be fair to my employers and true to myself. I did prevaricate, requesting to be moved to another department thinking it may just be the legal department that was becoming too routine, especially after over ten years of running the same department.

At my request, the Managing Director at the time, Disun Holloway, agreed that I hand the legal department to my deputy, Denike Laoye, whilst I started a new unit, the Private Banking Unit. I retained my position as Company Secretary. I ran the Private Banking Unit for a couple of years but the gnawing feeling didn't go away. So, again I took the very serious decision to leave when the ovation was loudest and chart my course as an entrepreneur. I resigned in August 2002 and was given a grand send-off cocktail by my bank in appreciation of my contributions to the bank since inception in 1989.

ARRIVING AT THE VISION AND EXPRESSING SAME

I had long made up my mind that whenever I left the bank, I would not go into private practice as a lawyer. I think I had seen the stress so many lawyers have to go through trying to get briefs from banks! Also, I honestly didn't have the deep passion for law that I know was required to sustain a lucrative practice. Many people suggested I enter into partnership with established firms or maybe even aspire for a position on the bench as a judge. However, none of these excited me. I was certain I needed to do "something" that I would enjoy and be happy to do even if I wasn't being paid for it!

I set out talking to friends and acquaintances who ran their own business, asking questions about how they started and how they grew. Everyone I spoke to had started off just doing something that they enjoyed, or something they were naturally good at, and their businesses came alive! So.... What was I good at? What came naturally to me? Easy: organizing things, influencing people. So how is that a business idea? Who will pay you to organize something for them? As the idea grew within my spirit I began to pray and talk to people about its possible viability. I tried to get books on the subject in England but wasn't very successful. Then a young friend, Ejiro Ajise, suggested we look on the internet. He went to amazon.com and came back to me with an incredibly long list of books on a subject which I wasn't even sure existed in the way I was thinking it through. I was able to get some of the books and I devoured them. Eureka! It can be done! It has been done in the USA, it is a thriving industry there and if they can do it I can do it. After all, the motto of my church

(The Fountain of Life Church) is "I can do ALL THINGS through Christ who strengthens me".

I need to acknowledge here three friends who really supported this vision and encouraged me to go out and do it. They are; Subu Giwa-Amu, Ayotola Ayodeji and Dele Ige. You are truly Eventful's Godmothers! I appreciate also my friend Julia Oku, who came up with the name "Eventful" under divine inspiration one day while we were fellowshipping and sharing thoughts. Julia is now known as Eventful's Grandma!

I also must recognize Mr. Akinsola Akinfemiwa, the M.D. of Skye Bank. He entrusted me with my very first event, for the then Prudent bank. That was well before event planners were accepted and recognized in corporate Nigeria as they are today. Mr. Akinfemiwa was saying "YES" to people's dreams long before his advertising agency in Skye Bank came up with that pay off line!

So now I had the BIG IDEA. What to do next? I prayed very hard. I needed to seek God's counsel and guidance on how to run with the vision. In my church, we have a tradition where you pick a scripture written on a small card at the beginning of every year. We call these "promises" and believe that God speaks to us through the promises. At the beginning of 2002 (the year I decided I would resign) the promise I picked was Psalm 128:2, it says, "When you eat the labour of your hands, you shall be happy, and it shall be well with you". WOW! God doesn't need to come down from heaven to talk to us. He speaks through His word. That was the assurance I needed that the time was now. It was time to "eat the labour of my hands", no longer that of any employer and God had declared that I would be happy and it would be well with me. And indeed, as always, God has been faithful to his word.

I was ready to resign that January. That was how excited I was! However, I had to wait a few more months because I was to share offices with my husband, Teni. He was in the process of acquiring a printing press at Ilupeju which would afford us more space. I was Executive Director in his company Zacchi & Krome Limited, and ideally the plan was for me to run my "little" events business on the side whilst supervising the administrative and Human Resource requirements of Zacchi & Krome. The first few months were rather quiet for Eventful and I was beginning to get worried that maybe Nigeria wasn't really ready for my "groundbreaking" ideas. Fortunately, the worst case scenario for me was that if it didn't take off, it would die a natural death and I would happily continue as ED in Zacchi & Krome and help build our family business, just as my mother had done with my father before me.

I need to go now into some detail here of how my value system, which is my Christian faith, impacted my business growth and success. I mentioned earlier that my very first event was organizing a product launch of sorts for Prudent Bank. The bank wanted to host a Christmas party for 3000 (yes 3000!) children who had opened the Children's Rainbow Savings Accounts. The purpose was also to attract prospective clients. This was in December 2001. I was still working for Ecobank but I took my annual vacation at that time and organized the event. I had planned to use the fees I received to pay for the incorporation of the events company I was about to start. Then one day

I was talking to my friend, Lamide Balogun, and she asked me what my plan was for the fees I would earn. I told her and she then asked if I knew about the principle of "first fruits". I was not that conversant with it and so she explained that I could sow the fees as a seed to God, being the very first fruits from a business venture I was praying would be successful. I needed no further persuasion. I believe the entire fee for the event was about N150,000.00. I wrote the cheque for the total sum to my church, explained what I was doing to my Pastor, Pastor Taiwo Odukoya. He prayed over my seed and I sowed cheerfully. I have no doubt in my mind that this seed made a way for me in this uncharted terrain and has brought me the incredible harvest of goodwill and abundance that I have enjoyed.

However, the first six months from October 2002 were still quite slow. But at least I had now employed a Personal Assistant and was trying my best to be CEO, Event Coordinator, Logistics Manager, Accountant etc etc all at the same time, and plodding along with one or two events a month.

Sometime in the first quarter of 2003, I experienced a significant turnaround. I attended a service in my church where a young man gave a testimony about how he had been giving significantly to the church building fund, and literally emptied his account in the process, and how God had really blessed him. I was so convicted by this testimony that I decided I must give in a more disciplined manner to the building fund instead of the sporadic way I was then doing. I thought I heard God say I should be giving 15% of my profit, and I was pleased. Of course I could do that.

But then the Holy Spirit said to me clearly, "50% my dear, not 15%"
"Get thee behind me, satan" I shouted! "How? 50% ke?"

I battled the matter down to the ground with the Holy Spirit in that service, but no prizes for guessing who won! I purposed in my heart that once I cleared the backlog of various debts I had then, I would begin to sow 50% of my profit to the building fund for the whole of 2003.

This was not an easy decision, nor was it easy to implement, but with the help of the Holy Spirit and the ever available grace of God, I did it. The unbelievable thing was that in spite of that sacrificial giving, I NEVER LACKED materially in any area of my life that year, and was able to do all I wanted to. It was obvious that God wanted me to prove to Him that this business is His and all glory would always be to Him.

Since the time I gave that offering, the growth of the business was phenomenal. I did not need to advertise. I never left my office in Ilupeju to market anyone. Clients would seek me out and ask for my services. The word of mouth referrals I got were amazing. My scriptural promise for the year 2003 was Isaiah 50:7, "For the Lord God will help me, therefore I will not be disgraced, therefore I have set my face like a flint, and I know that I will not be ashamed."

When business was a bit slow between late 2002 and early 2003, that word from God was my definite assurance that I would not fail. Having taken the bold step of faith to forsake the comforts of corporate life for the rigours of entrepreneurship in a difficult terrain, indeed I set my face like a flint, confident that I would not be disgraced by having to return shamefacedly to paid employment.

CHALLENGES ENCOUNTERED

Considering my family, academic and work background, I was clear in my mind that I wanted to run a first class company. I was, of course, sometimes uncertain how far I could take the vision, but as the business began to grow in terms of clientele, complexity, and demands, I resolved that, as far as was possible, I would run my company as professionally as I could.

The first challenge I encountered on leaving the bank was the incredibly insensitive comments of people who felt I was making a mistake and told me so. I heard comments such as "Ki lo gb'oju le o, o fi ise bank sile" (what does she depend on? What is her confidence that she left a well-paying bank job for this?). My answer to all of these was "God."

You will be amazed at the number of dream-killers that are amongst us. Some well-meaning people who couldn't see as far as I could even sat me down to tell me that with my qualifications and background how could I condescend to be organizing parties and events for people?!

Whilst my company focuses much more on corporate events, we have had the privilege of organizing several high society weddings and landmark birthdays, and I am as proud of the services I have rendered to those clients as I am of the many sophisticated conferences, seminars and corporate launches that we have organized for our corporate clients. There was a definite need for event planners - social and corporate - at this stage of our country's development, and our company provides a qualitative service that fills that gap.

I am glad that all the sceptics have been proven wrong. This is why you must be true to yourself and live your own life. If I was not, I would easily have been ensnared by these negative comments and given up on my dream, particularly in those not-so-busy earlier months. Now I have the privilege of my company being considered as the pioneer and market-leader in this field, thus opening up a new business venture for many other young entrepreneurs.

The second significant challenge I have faced is Human Resources. I decided very early that I could only work with people who were on the same wavelength as me. After struggling it out more or less alone for the first couple of years, it was clear that I needed people who could understand and run with the vision. The quality of graduates being turned out in Nigeria at the moment is absolutely appalling. I had discovered this development as far back as my days in Ecobank when so much training and reorientation had to be given to new staff to enable them deliver at the level expected of a regional bank. I am fortunate to have two excellent young women, Kofo Olawoyin and Evelyn Osinuga, leading my team of coordinators, and we are continually striving to nurture and mentor the junior coordinators. We celebrated our 5th anniversary recently and Kofo is now a partner in the company, whilst Evelyn is now Head of a new department, Eventful Weddings, which we set up in response to a growing demand that we organise weddings for our clients.

Events planning is essentially a passion, not a job. It's simply not for everyone. Finding the right mix of passion, intelligence, interpersonal skills, confidence, organisational skills and writing skills (for the tons of proposals we need to write) is a serious challenge! We seek to continually motivate and train our staff so they can deliver the quality of service that is expected of our company.

The state of infrastructure in the country is also an area of concern even in the service industry. The persistent lack of electricity has a significant effect on our bottom line at the end of each month. The state of the roads and the resultant traffic gridlocks affect our communication with our clients (thank God for email!). These however are challenges faced by all Nigerian businesses, small or large, so we will all continue with that struggle until our change comes, and come it surely will.

Probably the most significant challenge of running a small business is the great difficulty in establishing structure and corporate governance. I am fortunate that because of my background as a lawyer and company secretary I do keep records of all transactions, document everything and have a proper filing system. However, considering I was responsible for ensuring compliance in the bank for so many years I could not believe how non-compliant I was initially in terms of the status of my accounts, taxes and other regulatory requirements. Essentially, the business was growing so quickly and because I was wearing so many hats at the same time, I just never got round early enough to sorting out those issues.

Fortunately because of a project we were working on which required presenting financial statements, audited accounts etc, I quickly engaged the services of other professionals, accountants, and lawyers to help sort out our back office issues I am glad to say that we are now almost fully compliant and are now in the process of galvanizing our Board of Directors into active service. Professionalism is not only about the manner which your services are delivered but also the way your business is run.

Another thorny issue I have faced is that of gratification. Given my faith and what I have seen of the hand of God upon my life there are some things I know I cannot embark upon even though it appears to be the accepted norm in our terrain.

Fortunately I have a precedent set by my mentor in business, Mrs. Ibukun Awosika, CEO of Sokoa Chair Centre. Her company does not give or receive bribes and yet is probably the most successful indigenous furniture manufacturing company in Nigeria today. I took a deliberate decision to adopt this policy and have often found myself in the embarrassing position of trying to explain these convictions to well-meaning people who regard it as a natural course of business. God has given us grace so far and we believe that with the help of the Holy Spirit we will not let Him down. I am a firm believer in the greatness of this country Nigeria and I am certain that if one by one, each of us can strive for what is right, change will come to our land.

At Christmas, we appreciate, in our own small way, those who have contributed to our successes during the year. This we believe is appropriate and acceptable.

THE ROLE OF SPOUSE

I consider the role of one's spouse a critical success factor for a woman who wants to be successful in business. It is extremely important that we counsel the younger generation to choose their spouse with great care considering all the practical aspects of life, before tying the nuptial knot. Too many young girls are concerned with only the wedding and not the marriage (life after the wedding day!) If you want to be a great entrepreneur, which requires significant commitment of time and resources, there is no point in marrying a man who wants a housewife who will personally cook him hot meals everyday!

I am extremely fortunate to have been married to a man who truly supports my vision and helps to fulfil my dreams.

As I said earlier, Eventful started out within the premises of my husband's business. We started off by using one, then two, and three offices within the premises before we moved to our own business offices in 2006. I did not pay any rent or phone bills at that time because my husband was willing to support me.

Teni has always been the one with a flair for marketing, and he does a better job of marketing my business than I do any day! At any opportunity, he is pushing me to do better, travel further and take on challenges I would not even have considered if I didn't have his backing and support. A husband can either give his wife the wings to fly by his unconditional support or pull her down by making unreasonable demands that will not allow her express herself the way God has destined her to do.

Recently, while I was away on vacation, and my two senior coordinators were also in Abuja for two separate events, a new client called and requested for a meeting in respect of a conference to be held in Lagos. The junior coordinators were not really experienced enough to attend such a meeting on their own. I was completely blown away when my husband offered to go with them, so at least someone with some measure of authority (he is the Chairman of Eventful!) would be present at the meeting. And when he met with the client, the person turned out to be an old friend of his. So that went rather well!

You need to be able to share your passion and your vision with your life partner, so if you are yet to marry, please choose carefully. If you are already

41

married, apply God's wisdom to turn around your situation if it is not presently in your advantage.

Apart from my husband, my immediate family have always played a significant supportive role in my life. When I told my parents I wanted to leave the bank, there were no issues. All they wanted was for me to be happy and successful.

I received the unconditional support of the three figures of authority in my life, namely my parents, my husband and my pastors. The confidence they had in my abilities as a person, and God's faithfulness in my life propelled me to drive my vision to the fullest so as not to let any of them down.

As for my sisters Olufunto Olagbegi, Omobola Johnson, Ibiwunmi Akinnola and Arinola Kola-Daisi, they are my prayer partners and an incredible rock of support at all times. As far as they were concerned, I had successfully been managing the events of our lives from when we were young, so what's new? I am known as "ZachyEto" by my sisters because of my penchant for sorting everything out, whether they asked me to or not. A real busy-body elder sister!

My children Teniola and Iretidayo, whom I thought would see their mum more when I resigned from the bank, are the ones I really have to thank for their understanding. If you are a budding entrepreneur, listen well YOU DO NOT HAVE MORE TIME FOR YOURSELF WHEN YOU START YOUR OWN BUSINESS! You may be more flexible in the allocation of your time, but trust me, it will literarily take over your life at the early stages. If you are truly passionate about it, you will live, breathe and dream of that venture. Your life truly can never be the same again! But it is worth it when it begins to yield fruit, so persevere!

Recently my daughter said to me after an intense period of time when I had been working weekday nights and weekends back to back as well as travelling up and down the country. "Mummy, I feel so sorry for you. You are so tired! Why don't you just tell them at Eventful that you're not doing again jo"? Oh for the simplicity with which a child can view life!

My family are all extremely proud of my achievements to date, and I believe that the best is yet to come. My vision is to run a first class company, with a clear perspective of integrity, excellent service delivery and professionalism. Our pay-off line is that 'Eventful is creative, experienced and professional.' And we strive, God giving us the grace, to be all this. Clients trust us with significant amounts of money in order to provide a service that will enhance their event in a multifaceted manner and we strive to give value for money.

I believe that one's faith cannot be limited to where one worships; but must be pervasive, reflecting in one's relationships with people, lifestyle, and the manner and style of one's business. I ascribe every success Eventful has achieved over the past 5 years to God's hand being upon this company.

I am certain that the seeds I have sown have brought a legacy of success that I am only building on with hard work. I have paid my tithes for as long as I can remember and I faithfully tithe my company's profits also. The principles of God can never fail. I am confident that I am fulfilling the purpose for which I have been created by establishing and running this business, training and mentoring those who either come through my business or seek me as a mentor.

We successfully ran a training programme "So You Want to be an Event Manager?" in August 2007. This was well attended by over 30 people, including corporate affairs managers from banks and other companies, as well as upcoming and established Event Planners. Participants were all grateful for an opportunity to brainstorm and share challenges and issues faced in an emerging industry.

We have compiled the materials delivered at that training programme into a manual, a step by step guide for those who wish to pursue a career in event management. The entry barrier to the event management business is minimal, as no qualifications are actually required for you to call yourself an events manager. We have therefore decided to harness our experience and provide this manual to assist those coming after us. Why? If we all get better the professional standards will be raised and this can only be good for us all in the long run.

I believe I am adding value and I continue to seek for inspiration from the Holy Spirit for direction on what to do next to take the business to the next level. We are now venturing into the establishing and management of event venues. We are constantly challenged in our business by the dearth of venues in Lagos, when organizing events for our clients. We have decided that this is the next phase to conquer. An opportunity to acquire prime land and begin this project came up recently. I believe that the God that has brought us this far will not leave us or forsake us, no matter, how incredulous the mind-boggling sums of money that is required for this new vision may seem.

I pray my story has encouraged someone to go out and DO IT, EVEN IF YOU ARE AFRAID!

BOLANLE AUSTEN-PETERS

2

Name:
BOLANLE AUSTEN-PETERS
(NEE BABALOLA)

Name of Company:
TERRA KULTURE

Post:
MANAGING DIRECTOR

INDUSTRY:
ARTS & CULTURE

BACKGROUND

My childhood was normal and filled with good memories. My siblings and I had a good upbringing under the love and tutelage of our parents. I was the last of my mother's children, but this did not earn me any special privilege, certainly not with my very strict Dad

My Dad, a lawyer, is a highly principled and disciplined person. He therefore instilled in us those values. He is a disciplinarian and he trained us all to be focused. He gave us room to be free with him, and to always express our views on issues. He raised us to be independent and taught us to strive to do the best of our abilities in anything we set out to do. For instance, if we asked for money, he would remind us that by age eighteen in Europe, you were expected to be independent, and living by yourself. He wanted us to be able to face challenges, and be able to think things through on our own.

My Mum worked with the medical corps of the Nigerian military and that informed my love for men/women in uniform. My Mum developed my interest in sports. I swim, cycle, play tennis, badminton, squash, and volleyball.

My father also enjoyed farming and we own a large farm in the village and in our house in Ibadan. I love farming. The joy of watching a seed grow is phenomenal. The open air and outdoor space all add to my joy of farming. My Mum also owned a poultry and we would clean it every Saturday.

My childhood was definitely fun and I cherish my memories of it. In particular, I cherish the grounding my parents provided.

My primary education was at Mary Hill Covenant School, Ibadan and Command Children School, Ann's Barracks, Lagos. From there, I went to Command Secondary School, Ibadan and International School, Ibadan. I studied Law at the University of Lagos and obtained a Masters degree in International Law from the London School of Economics and Political Science. I also enrolled in a number of courses whilst working with the United Nations in different capacities.

Law wouldn't have been my first choice course, even though my Dad encouraged us to study professional courses so we could be on our own, but my Mathematics wasn't that great. I would have preferred studying History. Anyhow, I ended up with Law and specialized in international law because I saw an avenue for adventure in it and an opportunity to touch lives.

WORK EXPERIENCE AND BIRTH OF VISION

I worked in my dad's law firm for about a year and a half before joining the United Nations where I worked with the Centre for Human Rights. I was transferred to the United Nations High Commission for Refugees, and then later to the UNDP. It was indeed a lot of fun being with the UNHCR, though it was not without its rigours. The job entailed a lot of travelling and sometimes we had to work under critical conditions. I worked in remote places with refugees. We travelled a lot through East Africa. It was exciting, novel, and sometimes dangerous.

I also worked in Geneva and Namibia before relocating back to Nigeria.

I returned as a Consultant to the UNDP, but I soon realized that I needed to do something more socially relevant and interesting. I began to feel restless and thinking of an area where I could make a difference and have a positive impact.

I observed that a lot of children were not speaking Nigerian languages, and based on this I chose to put together a project that would focus on teaching Nigerian languages. This was the genesis of Terra Kulture. I later expanded the project to include our culture, arts, music and food. Basically, what we do in Terra Kulture is to define the Nigerian identity by creating an environment where both Nigerians and foreigners can learn about Nigerian arts and culture.

So you can say I arrived at the vision that led to the birth of Terra Kulture on my observation of a dearth of space to promote Nigerian culture, food, arts, and the entire Nigerian heritage. In addition, I wanted to create jobs for people, and thereby reduce the rate of unemployment in our society.

SETTING UP

Towards setting up the establishment, the first thing I did was to discuss my idea with my husband. My brother in-law also helped in putting together my financials. Since I was going to venture into a very unique industry, one that was not so common in the country, I needed his advice and, most especially, his support to brave the journey.

Once assured of his support, I proceeded to write a business plan which served as a roadmap and helped me organize how I would go about setting up the business in measurable steps. Then I started looking for the required funding to start up from different corporate organizations. I met with the MD of GTBank who could relate to the vision. After all that was put in place, Terra Kulture came into being.

I love reading. So in order to be successful at what I have chosen to do, I also invested time and money reading a lot of books and sourcing information relevant to my field. I also went online and did a lot of research.

It took me about eight months of discussing with people and writing out my business plan before I could finally start off.

CHALLENGES

The reality is that when you start a business, initially your personal life will suffer. There is nothing that can be done to mitigate that. However, as the business begins to settle, you need to work out a balance. Different businesses have different gestation periods and what would work for A would not necessarily work for B. The bottom line is that you need to find that balance. I started finding the balance after two years of running the business. For others it could be more or less. What is sure though, is that the balance has to be found, otherwise, other facets of one's life will begin to suffer. In my case, my health was the first pressure point.

My greatest challenge in running the business has been the lack of skilled staff. Today, we find that with the falling standards in education and general societal values, getting skilled staff is increasingly difficult. Most graduates have never had the opportunity of working before their first paid job. This means that you have to teach them literally everything.

The work ethic in Nigeria is also very poor and most people do not understand the notion of literally earning your wages. People work only if they are supervised or watched. Things would be left undone except you specifically delegate and follow up. This invariably burdens the proprietor or business owner. It also goes without saying that as a young business, you are most probably not able to recruit skilled staff even when available.

The other challenge that ranks on the same scale with the above is the lack of basic infrastructure to run a business. We, as a company, have had to take on the statutory responsibilities of the government. Please note that as things stand, we are levied nothing less than ten different taxes annually. Yet, we are still responsible for generating our own electricity, water, security, drainage, etc. We have had to invest valuable seed money into purchasing two generators which also come with their own associated overheads (maintenance and fuelling).

Meanwhile, we still pay PHCN bills every month. We had to provide our own water by sinking boreholes, and we also have to pay excessive amounts for security. The list goes on, but it is sufficient to note that the government needs to create an enabling environment for business to thrive; otherwise these costs invariably prevent most businesses from succeeding, let alone make profit.

My major growth challenge at the moment is getting skilled staff who will connect with the vision, and thus find it easy to understand the very essence of the enterprise. I am also contending with the issue of getting good advertising that will tell our story in the way that it will appeal to our audience.

SPOUSAL/FAMILY SUPPORT
My husband has been very supportive of me in the venture. As a matter of fact, he has always been

there for me from the very onset of the business. I really don't know how I would have fared without his constant support and encouragement. I have always been drawing from his ceaseless counsel on different ways to run my business. He also assisted me a great deal in terms of financial and emotional support.

From experience, I consider the role of the spouse in actualizing an entrepreneurial dream to be extremely important. Besides, there is an extent a woman can go without the support of her husband. There is a need to have someone to rely on at all times, whether it's a husband, a close friend or a relative.

In my evolution in business, my family has played and is still playing a very positive role. Their influence, in terms of encouragement and support, has been what kept me moving on when the road gets rough. They have a strong belief in my ability, as a woman, to actualize my dreams and visions.

Nigerian women are held from achieving greatness by self-imposed societal and religious beliefs. In view of this, Nigerian women need to break free of these beliefs. They need to be more involved in nation building and politics. They need to be more involved in wealth acquisition. This is very critical because it is only when you have attained some level of economic independence that you can begin to think of affecting the lives of those around you.

Those who choose to be housewives can also contribute to the development of the nation by enforcing a deep sense of values and discipline in their children because this is what instils the moral fibre that will carry them through life.

I think my core values as a Christian defines me as a person. I am greatly challenged by the extreme poverty in our society. I look around daily and ask myself, how can I contribute to this society? How can I positively impact other people's lives? This is what motivates and inspire me. I constantly try to take myself out of my comfort zone and imagine the life of the average Nigerian. The thought alone makes me want to be the best I can be. If the only way I can create an impact is by creating jobs howbeit difficult for me to do, it is worth taking the risk.

I would like to be an asset to my community, but most importantly, I would like to create jobs. We talk daily about unemployment but the reality of the matter is that government alone cannot create all the jobs needed. Private sector involvement is required. We are the people that can complement the efforts of the government.

My candid opinion is that in a country like ours which is still developing, if you are fortunate to come from a background that has provided you with the needed exposure and skills, you have no business staying in paid employment. You need to create jobs for others and not wait to be employed. It is scary, yes. However, with the right spirit, fortitude and vision, it is achievable. If each of us were to make it our personal target to recruit a certain number of persons in a year, unemployment would be greatly reduced and we would be all the better for it because crime and other societal malaise would considerably reduce.

ROLE MODEL
I have come to see every successful person in business as a veritable model to learn from.

VALUE SYSTEM
My value systems are wrapped in my strong faith in God, and in the possibility of all things through God. I have learnt the tenet of having a strong focus in whatever I do in life. I also believe in a lot of hard work.

To this end, I pray a lot. So whenever I am feeling down, I have always found prayers to be my refuge. This is one way I have immensely benefited from my value system. My family values have also helped me as well, as it has given me a lot of support. Right from my childhood, I have learnt the value of honesty, dedication and hard work in my family, plus a lot of work ethic as well.

EXITING STRATEGY
My exit strategy: I have a board in place that is the final decision making body in the company. My

staff undergo training that will stretch and bring out the very best in them, for now and for future challenges. Finally, I have a deputy who has been well groomed in all the rudiments and operations of the business, who can easily take over from me without the company suffering any major loss as a result of my not been there.

At the end of my days, I would like to be remembered as someone who worked and loved working hard. I will also like to be remembered as one who had faith in God; as well as someone who contributed to the growth of Nigeria.

BETTY IRABOR

3

Name:
BETTINA IRABOR
(NEE BELO-OSAGIE)

Name of Company:
GENEVIEVE MAGAZINE

Post:
CEO/EDITOR-IN-CHIEF

INDUSTRY:
PUBLISHING

BACKGROUND-THE EARLY YEARS

I was born as Betty Belo-Osagie and raised in Lagos. A passion for the arts had been deeply embedded in my heart from my early days. My mother was a dressmaker, a vocation which requires a certain level of creativity, and this served as a strong influence on my life. My interest in books and poetry since my childhood days was a breeding point for my passion in writing. So while I was growing up, I had dreams of going into sports, as well as to become an author.

Being the second in a family of five children, and raised by a single mum, I grew up to be a very strong woman, and always prided myself, just like my sisters, as focused.

I attended Methodist Girls High School where I did my O' levels and, subsequently, my A' levels from 1971 to 1977. I then moved on to study English and philosophy at the University of Lagos. As a great lover of sports, I represented my school in athletic hurdles championships and also represented Lagos state at state championships as well.

After my degree, like every average Nigerian graduate, I went job-hunting and was employed by an advertising company. After a stint there, I got a job in The National Concord. This was my first experience with the pen on a professional level and the beginning of my career as a journalist. My work as a journalist\features writer earned me the description of a prolific writer by my superiors.

I left The National Concord for the corporate world in 1988 where I worked at Haisha Investment Company as a Public Relations/Administration Manager for two years before I resigned to team up with my husband, Soni Irabor, as the CEO of Ruyi Communications. During this time my flair for writing did not go without expression as I freelanced for a number of newspapers such as This Day, Vanguard, and Guardian, amongst others.

It was in the course of my new posting as the CEO of Ruyi Communications that I started my entrepreneurial journey as the Editor-In-Chief of Genevieve Magazine.

The Vision- GETTING STARTED

As the saying goes, "life begins at forty." I got a wake-up call when, at the age 40, I looked at my life in retrospect. It has been a good and enviable life thus far, but there still remained an unidentified yearning in me that longs to be fulfilled. Five years later, I saw a magazine called Female, it was a lifestyle magazine published in Singapore. And as I glanced through its pages the spark that lit the Genevieve vision was born!

To prevent the vision from fizzling out as a passing fancy, I earnestly started working on it. I began by creating a dummy of the magazine and then sampling the opinions of my family and friends on it. The magazine was named Genevieve in honour of my daughter who was named after St. Genevieve.

From the onset, the values that would govern the publication were defined, as well as the principles on which every story would be based. It was to be a wholesome magazine, which reflects and celebrates the values of the total woman. According to a business plan drawn up by my consultant, a large amount of money was needed to successfully run the magazine. Having some money in the bank, I set out in search of investors for the magazine. My passion and unshaken belief in what I was doing inspired investors to invest in the magazine. Rather than invest a lot of money into the business at once, I decided to invest in proportion to the growth of the business.

Another important step I took was to inaugurate a board for the purpose of checks and balances. I also instituted an advisory board, which consisted of respected media personnel such as Sam Amuka Pemu, Doyin Abiola, and Dr Bello Osagie, amongst others. While all these were being done, I also began a search for a staff of vision-carriers who would work with me.

CHALLENGES

There was no template to use as a benchmark, and that was the biggest challenge for Genevieve initially. There were no glossy magazines at the time; so my team and I had to work on a fresh canvass and developed a template with nothing to use as a reference. Another challenge we faced was getting a good press outfit for the printing of the publication. A research was therefore carried out to solve this problem and this resulted in quotations being sent in from printing outfits in South Africa, America and Nigeria. And because I did not have too much money to play with, putting in mind the costs of printing abroad, shipment, and other import tariffs, we decided that the magazine be printed locally.

Apart from the task of having to put a workable publishing office together from the scratch, I also had to contend with the challenges of infrastructural deficiencies, inconsistent power supply and other national issues that affect Nigerian industries. There was also the challenge of meeting deadlines, getting the photography and the content right, winning the confidence of sources or interviewees and getting advertisers.

As common to all publishers, circulation was a major challenge I had to battle with at inception. Then, in the process of time, more lifestyle glossies were published and the issue of competition also set in. This caused an impressive drive amongst the Genevieve team. We were set to pursue and achieve our dreams beyond people's expectations.

For the first two years, there was a problem with the financial structure of the magazine. At the initial stage, there was no need for a defined structure, but as the business grew the need became clearer. As a result of this financial structural defects, the magazine lost part of its profit. In order to solve this problem, I employed a financial manager and with time, a good financial structure was put in place.

FAMILY ROLE

I am married to a loving and supportive husband who stood by me through the painstaking stages of birthing a lifestyle magazine like Genevieve. He would personally hawk the magazine whenever we were lodging in Hotels like Nicon Hilton and fondly referred to me as a world-class publisher even when this wasn't the case then. He was very understanding when I had to edit till late in the night or supervised production works. At times when I was editing till as late as 2.00a.m, he would sit beside me and offer to help in any way he could. And when the toll of being a model publisher started to set in, he was always there for me.

I am a proud mother of two, and my family served as a mini advisory board supporting and criticizing every of my ideas for the magazine. They fully understand the importance of this dream to me and willingly stand by me. They serve as a source of strength and they are my loudest fans. Even when sacrifices had to be made and the company took my topmost attention, my family viewed things from an understanding perspective rather than being resentful.

VALUE SYSTEM

The vision I have for Genevieve is for it to be the number one magazine for women of all ages, the men in their lives, as well as to inspire the Nigerian woman to embrace her authentic self. To see a woman complete, confident and inspired to be all she can be is my heart-cry and the essence of the Genevieve magazine.

As a staunch believer in God, I am a stickler for integrity, honesty, fair play and a consistent pursuit of excellence, amongst other godly values. And all these lie at the core of Genevieve's establishment. As a result, certain principles were set on editorial and advertorial content. The ethos of the magazine is to inspire women and point a beacon of hope that will empower and motivate them in their quest for a stylish, balanced and healthy lifestyle.

In promoting physical, mental and spiritual balance amongst our readers, the content range spreads across features, human stories, health, beauty, style, politics, fitness, finance etc. The importance and value of delivering a wholesome magazine is taken to heart at Genevieve, and this I do relentlessly. As a result, Genevieve has carved a niche for itself, creating a brand that cannot be refuted in the media publishing industry.

GROWTH CHALLENGES

The growth challenge that Genevieve is facing is a good one; it is the problem of more demand than supply. Our readership is like a cult, and some loyal readers don't always get to buy their copies before it is sold out! The circulation is also a challenge; that is getting the magazine to the readers within their convenience.

Like most entrepreneurial establishments, I appear to be the most passionate and visible figure in the company, and therefore get the most recognition. However, I look forward to a day when the magazine will become far bigger than me. And I believe that with investment from more investors the magazine would go to the stock exchange.

Another growth challenge we are facing is living up to the expectation of our readers. When you become a model and a respected brand, everyone looks up to you. It's like climbing up a mountain, the higher you go, the harder it becomes.

HANDOVER STRATEGY

In the seventh year of my marriage, I had a baby girl christened Sonia Irabor. She has been a major support and pillar since the magazine's inception. She shares my creativity and passion about the magazine, and was the magazine's youngest contributor at the initial stages. She is currently studying media communication abroad, and she majors in publishing in preparation to take over the management of the company from me at the appropriate time.

At the time of my exit, I hope to be remembered as a woman who inspired others to follow their dreams, find their purpose, and know that it is never too late to live their dreams.

I believe it is never over for anyone, whenever you wake up, is your morning!

TARA FELA-DUROTOYE

4

Name:
TARA FELA-DUROTOYE
(NEE SAGAY)

Name of Company:
HOUSE OF TARA

Post:
CREATIVE DIRECTOR

Industry:
COSMETICS & STYLES

BACKGROUND

I was born on 6 March 1977 at St. Nicholas Hospital, as Mewe Tara Sagay, to Mr John Ejegi Sagay and Mrs Felicia Omaghomi. The union did not last long, for they separated when I was only eight months old. So I was brought up by my father's wife, Mrs Modupe Agnes Sagay, from the age of eight.

Due to the fact that my father was polygamous, I had another step-mother as well. Childhood was not very exciting for me, as I was the only biological child of both my parents. My stepmother, Modupe Agnes did a great job of making me happy. However, I was happy to leave the house for a boarding school, and so away from the taunting of my other stepmothers.

I started my education at Command Children's School, Victoria Island, and then proceeded to the Nigerian Navy Secondary School, Ojo, an outskirt of Lagos. There, at my form one, I met with the Lord Jesus Christ, and that made the pains of polygamy and separation of my parents easier for me to bear. And the experience was soothing enough that I was willing to return home from the boarding house in my form three.

I became the Sanitary and Welfare Prefect in form 5 and developed my faith and ability to transfer the knowledge of biblical principles to other students at that time. I consider this phase of my life self-identifying and very refreshing indeed. Besides, it prepared me for where I am today. I developed strong leadership traits, coupled with a desire to succeed. I also came to realise that I was not just an ordinary girl, but a person of influence.

One of the dreams I had then was to become a successful lawyer who specialises in international Law, and who could speak both French and Spanish. I desired to study at Cambridge University in the United Kingdom, which happens to be my father's Alma Mater. I also desired to work at the Rotimi Williams & Co. chambers so as to develop my skills. I had a stint of working experience assisting the clerks in one of the courts at the Federal High Court on Queen's Drive (now Oyinkan Abayomi drive) for some months before going into the University. I got this job simply by my own efforts.

There I developed my social skills the more because I met a number of lawyers that I interacted with. And as I grew older my father enrolled me at the Alliance Françoise on Kingsway road, Ikoyi, as well as the famous ICL computer school, in furtherance of my determination to become a successful international lawyer. I had this vision firmly in mind and everyday I was taking steps to actualise them. Although some of the things I was doing did not seem to make much sense to me at the time, now I realised that these traits were being developed in me for a time as this.

My dream came to an abrupt halt when my father had a stroke. And that meant I would not be going to the United Kingdom to further my studies as I had planned. This was a great blow to all my numerous dreams. And as I had not even made an alternative arrangement to study in Nigeria, it was indeed a great shock to my entire system.

My father had to retire as a commissioner at the federal civil service, and we had to move out of our comfortable house at Ikoyi to a smaller apartment.

Prior to this time I had never lived in a small house or a flat before, without all the perks that come with the official accommodation of a top government official that my father was. So in response to this new development, I made a decision never to be caught unaware at any point again in my life. I also made a resolution to be independent and build my own in life so that I would lack nothing.

Shortly thereafter, I got a job at Priscilla Ihenacho's perfumery, the only perfume and cosmetic shop at the time. It was a beautiful store; and while there I began to learn all I could and develop some of the skills that I later came to apply in my own business. After a year and half, I was ready to resume my education. So I got admission into Lagos State University to study Law. After one year of studying Law, and the death of my father in the second year, all my interests to work as a Lawyer disappeared. I then started to try my hands at different businesses. And after several trials, I finally settled for my present calling, that is running a beauty company.

I started the business, first as a bridal makeup artist by going the extra mile each day to offer my services to as many people as possible. Sometimes I did so even without charging a fee. Every time people saw me doing this, they complimented my works, and the more I did, the more people talked about me and my business to other people, and the more referrals I got. In consistency, I was able to see other opportunities from bridal makeup; it evolved in makeup school and makeup studio and the company has now evolved into manufacturing its own makeup line "Tara Orekelewa" which is being used to empower young ladies within the university community.

I really cannot say that I had any vision in mind when I started the business, save for the decision I made earlier which served as the fire that kept me going. But sometime later, my vision became articulated after I had attended several courses, out of my desire to build a sustainable business that will outlive me.

I started with a desire to be independent and make a name for myself, and building on this desire I went for several courses to give my desire a direction. I also read a lot of books. And this helped me to come up with a mission statement for the company as well as to create systems and structures. I also did role descriptions and assign duties to every individual in my team.

I formed a board of directors of eight persons, with only two of them being members of my family. I drafted a company policy document, which consisted of what the vision of the company is, and how we plan to actualise that vision. It also contained the code of conduct within the organisation, the culture and the way we relate to our customers, how we answer the phone etc. We also put in place accounting systems, an external auditor, accounting software, payment vouchers for petty cash, creating budgets etc.

I created departments within the company: such as Accounts/Admin, Human Resource, Business Development, Branding and Customer Retention etc. Then we began to organise training sessions for staff in management positions, and I expended a great deal of time in sharing the vision of the company with members of staff. Those who did not comply with the vision were fired.

The challenges I encountered in the course of starting up; first, my business was new in Nigeria. So I didn't have a model whose footsteps I could follow for direction because of the uniqueness of the profession. Then I also nursed the fear of people not accepting me or the ideas I came up with.

I also faced the challenge of getting members of staff to buy into my personal and corporate vision for the business. So that they will not see the company as a one-man business that will rise and die with the owner, without anything for them in it, especially when I wanted to start manufacturing my own brand of cosmetics. I also suffered lack of loyalty from some members of staff and betrayal from other people.

My family have always been supportive of my dream, from my parents to my sisters, Juliet and Caroline, who have always been a source of stability personally and for the business. But most of all, I am most grateful to my husband who was a business consultant at that time and therefore gave me "free" advice, consulted with me, and gave me the liberty to dream. I fondly remember that whenever I am sharing my ideas with him, he always puts an international perspective to it without the limitations of the 'Nigerian factor'.

I believe a spouse will either mar or make an entrepreneur. Entrepreneurship entails a lot of risk-taking; it involves taking a lot of unknown steps that one does not know where they may lead one to. And in order to take the necessary bold step you always need some support and the encouragement of a loved one, whom you are assured will be there for you come what may. This support enables you to be focused on the vision. For without being focused on your vision the chances are that they will not be actualised.

I consider Mary Kay Ash as my role model simply because of her style of running business. As a social entrepreneur, she has been able to combine her call to people and at the same time developing her firm to be one of the top 10 beauty companies in the world.

My business decisions are based on my Christian faith. I also see my business as a channel for propagating the kingdom of God.

My business has prospered as a result of my applying the biblical principles of hard work, tithing, focus, firstfruits, among others, all which form the core of my value system. They are indicators that anyone can apply to ensure success in business or any other endeavour in life.

Talking about my exit/handing over strategy; I have given myself a retirement date. And to that effect, I started grooming two successors who would possibly take over from me; one of them has left the company. But the other one is still with us and is still undergoing training in preparation for this position. The interesting thing about this is that they are both unaware of what I am doing.

At the end of my days, and on my exit, I will like to be remembered as someone whose story was an inspiration to many people; and also as one whose life is worthy of emulation, as a Christian, as a wife, and as a mother.

IFEYINWA IGHODALO

5

Name:
IFEYINWA IGHODALO
(NEE CHIGBO)

Name of Company:
DESIGN OPTIONS LTD

Post:
DIRECTOR/PARTNER

Industry:
FURNITURE

BACKGROUND

I am the first of three children, the only girl, and the first grandchild of my grandparents on both sides. As a result, I was made aware of my responsibilities from a very early age.

That notwithstanding, I had a fun-filled and very playful childhood. My family travelled around a lot and by the age of twelve I had lived in various parts of Nigeria and in several different countries around the world. I had all the various 'career' dreams that most young girls have. First, I wanted to be a nun, because of the long-flowing habit. Then, I wanted to be a nurse like my mother, but most likely because I thought the uniform cute, then a teacher, and sometimes maybe even a ballerina. Finally, when my father started his MBA course in the United States and under his gentle tutelage, I decided that I would eventually own and run my own business. I wasn't sure what line of business I wanted to pursue, but I knew I was going to own a successful business, by His Grace!

I was blessed with a quick and retentive mind and went through my primary and secondary education at home and abroad at the top of my class. I chose to study accounting as a first degree because of my love for and skill with mathematical figures, and as a foundation for my career in business. Whilst in the university, I discovered my interest in interiors. I found that I enjoyed arranging and rearranging the meagre furniture in my hostel room, bringing in various items of soft furnishing, playing with the paint colours on the wall and nurturing my indoor plants. Friends and other college mates often stopped by to actually view my room and compliment me on the décor.

I slowly began to realise that I actually enjoyed "playing" with décor. By the end of my four-year course in accountancy, it was clear to me that I would never work as an accountant. The exciting world of creative interiors beckoned.

I graduated with honours and with the help of my father was able to secure a job in a bank for my National Youth Corps Service (NYSC). This only helped to reaffirm my previous decision not to pursue a career in accountancy. Once my youth service was over, I immediately set out to fulfil my dream.

It wasn't easy convincing my father to sponsor my education in this new field mainly because he wanted me to practise as a chartered accountant or become a banker. Eventually though, I got him to agree and subsequently set out for an 18-month interior design course in London. While in London, I realised that, based on the course content, I would have done better studying furniture manufacturing rather than interior design, This was because at this time in Nigeria's development, not only was the importation of furniture banned, it was impossible to find locally manufactured furniture of the standard required for the kind of interiors I was intending to create on my return home to Nigeria.

I returned to Nigeria and decided that the provincial city of Enugu was too small for me to make my mark in my new vocation as a furniture manufacturer. There were no decent furniture manufacturers in Enugu. Yet again, I convinced my parents to permit me to relocate to Lagos as a young spinster. They agreed on one condition; that I secured a job first, rather than move to Lagos to set up my business as was my youthful plan.

I got a job with Casafina Nigeria Ltd in 1985 as their first Showroom Manager. Having worked in my parents furniture company COONITA on and off while at the university, and for about a year after my Youth Service, I brought a lot of my experience to bear in the setting up of the showroom space and layout for Casafina. This format was to be repeated in my own company when I finally set up a few years later.

It was while working in Casafina that I met Moni Omidiji who was to become my business partner. We had a shared vision of what the interior design and furniture landscape in Nigeria should look like, and we soon discovered that that vision was not shared by the owners of Casafina. So in October 1987, at the ages of 27 and 24 we both left and founded DESIGN OPTIONS LTD.

We started by handling soft furnishing, re-upholstery of furniture, and window treatments ourselves and subcontracting the actual production of furniture to established furniture makers. We soon discovered, however, that in order to really make the impact we wanted to, we had to first of all control the lead time for and quality of the production of our furniture; and secondly have a free hand in the choice of the designs to be produced.

We soon decided to set up our own mushroom or cottage furniture manufacturing workshop at Fadeyi, on the Lagos mainland. Prior to this time, we had been operating from both my spinster apartment at Yaba and out of our cars. Our clients were mostly expatriates living in Apapa, Ikoyi or Victoria Island, with a phobia for 'travelling' to the mainland.

Due to this their reluctance to come to the mainland, we found that we were constantly on the move going to both the offices and the homes of our clients, not just for the briefs but also for the execution of the jobs.
The next step was therefore to acquire a showroom where we could display our beautiful

products and have our customers come to us rather than we having to go to them all the time. At this point in our business and for many long years, the business had been financing itself. The banks were not interested in lending as a way of helping their customers. They were more often than not, and still are, only interested in attracting huge deposits from their customers.

For this reason, we were only able to set up a small showroom at Onikan, where we remained for years. Our numerous attempts to raise finance from our bankers in order to relocate and expand the business were repeatedly met with doors closing in our faces. We had no choice but to plough back all our profits and build up the capital required for the expansion of our business on our own.

Finally, in 2001, we were able to afford a much larger and more strategically located showroom on Victoria Island. The acquisition of a showroom with a lot of space resulted in an overnight explosion in our business. In order to keep up with the demands thrust on us by the sudden and rapid growth of the business, my partner and I enrolled for business courses at the Lagos Business School. These courses gave us a totally new outlook on how to run our business. We had started out as two young ladies with no formal, training. I, with my accounting background, had dabbled into furniture in my father's company; but my partner was a graduate with no prior business experience. We just shared a common dream and vision. LBS opened up to us a new way of looking at business in general and Design Options in particular. One of my regrets now is that having attended those courses about three years ago, I have not found the time to go back. I hope to make the time to correct this oversight in the near future.

The next thing we did was to start working with a team of consultants toward the re-engineering, restructuring and reorganization of our business in order to keep up with its rapidly growing demands. The business was moving from being a small-scale company to medium-scale enterprise. We had started as two persons, and had grown to a company employing over 100 people. We therefore needed to restructure in order to accommodate this growth. The first consultants we worked with was Accenture. At that time, they had this backroom programme, where they helped small and medium scale companies to tidy up all their backroom work so that they could focus on their core competence. Before we could conclude with Accenture they set up a subsidiary company called Chrysalis to handle the issues of small and medium scale companies. Once more, before we could go very far with the programme the company shut down. After all the time and effort we had invested in the programme over a period of about two to three years, it was quite a set back that affected our plans for reengineering and created unnecessary demands on the directors' time. This challenge was a greater one than the challenge of finance which we had previously faced. Finding the right management consultant afterwards was a major issue, many came to us but we quickly and painfully discovered they could not deliver.

Finally though, with continuous perseverance we seem to be nearing the end of this part of our journey.

It took us almost 17 years in business, after we had patronized various banks, before we finally found one that was friendly and supportive enough to be willing to grant us a facility to further expand our business. We had acquired two plots of land at Ilupeju where we wanted to build our factory, so with the facility we were able to do this.

I remember we once had a Local Purchasing Order (LPO) from Shell Petroleum and we put in an application for a facility in our bank of ten years, which they sent to their head office. We got their reply six months later, four months after we had completed the job!

The second major challenge we faced and are still facing is the calibre of the workforce available in

Nigeria now. Education has been non-existent in this country now for almost twenty years. So even with the work systems and procedures clearly defined, we still find that we have to teach our staff the basic rudiments of the tasks. Simple basics like Telephone manners, letter writing, and how to follow simple instructions.

The other challenges we have faced have been the unpredictability and exotic nature that characterise the policies of our government; the non-availability of adequate infrastructure and, most debilitating has been, the absence of a proper work ethic, coupled with the high degree of incompetence of the available manpower, as I previously stated. We have tried to overcome this last challenge by organising various training programmes, regularly brainstorming with our staff and encouraging feedback sessions. As well as by developing clearly defined and well documented work processes and procedures.

The federal government ban on importation of furniture would have constituted a challenge to us.

But ban or no ban, we have always been a manufacturing company.

Have our spouses been supportive in the business? I will say a big Yes! When Moni and I started our business, we were both spinsters, though we were then in relationships with our future mates. Both our spouses have turned out to be our major assets, pillars of strength and encouragement. They are sources of inspiration and literally the "wind beneath our collective wings!' Nothing is too little or too great for them to do for us in the realisation of our dreams. They have been our biggest networkers, sources of referrals, our PR machinery, and even our arbitrators in periods when the going got a little tough. Without them, we can honestly say, Design Options would not be where it is today.

I have had various mentors along the way, both personal and in business. One of my greatest mentors, apart from my husband and my father, is Mr. Fola Adeola. I admire his vision in establishing Guaranty Trust Bank (GTB), his relationship with his partner and his exit strategy. I have at various times gone to him for advice and the solution he proffered have been invaluable. Other mentors and models who have had a great influence on my business and personal life are Dr. Christopher Kolade and his wife Beatrice.

My father started me on the road to entrepreneurship. He taught me the principles of break-even analysis at the tender age of twelve. He also taught me the invaluable lesson of goodwill in business. To me, goodwill is the greatest asset any business concern can have. From day one, we have made that our watchword at Design Options, our word is our bond.

Our core value system in Design Options is a roadmap that leads to the pride we have in our good name. In Design Options, Honesty, Quality, Innovation, Commitment, Timeliness, Consistency and Team-spirit are the hallmark of our operations and dealings. The bottom line is that our customers, over the years, can rely on us to deliver often over and beyond their greatest expectations.

This is our 20th year in business. As we celebrate our 20th anniversary, our focus is geared strongly towards the fine-tuning and implementation of the executive management structure that we have been actively putting in place over the past five years, as a prelude to handing over.

Both of us, along with our staff team of 120, have worked long and very hard to create the brand that is Design Options. We would like our name to be synonymous with beautiful and innovative interiors, as well as exquisite and well-manufactured international standard furniture.

Personally, I would like to be remembered as a Nigerian woman who made a difference.

MONI FAGBEMI

6

Name:
MONI FAGBEMI
(NEE OMIDIJI)

Name of Company:
DESIGN OPTIONS

Post:
Director/PARTNER

Industry:
FURNITURE

BACKGROUND

I grew up at Ilupeju in an almost all-girls family in the mid 1960's. I am the second of three sisters and one brother, with just a year age-difference among we girls. We were popularly called 'the Omidiji girls" everywhere we went. Ours was an extremely happy home, with lots of fights, laughs, and sharing among one another. My dad was a very strict person, and we used to disappear whenever we heard the sound of his car driving into the compound from work.

After my O'levels here in Nigeria, our parents decided to send my sisters and I to England for some international exposure. It was a bit difficult being away from home for the first time in my entire sixteen years. However, we all ended up at the same school, Kent College for girls at Pembury Tunbridge Wells (which also happens to be my mum's alma mater between 1952 and 1956).

After two years, on completing our 'A Levels, we returned to Lagos to the "prestigious" University of Lagos and stayed in the "famous", interesting (but crazy) Moremi Hall. We didn't really mind having to return home for tertiary education so much because it was a good university (at that time), and all our friends were returning home as well.

At this stage, I personally had no 'clue' as to what I wanted to do with my life or what was in store for me. Nevertheless, I ended up doing a three year course in Social Science which I considered extremely boring throughout my time there.

After graduation, I decided to follow the general exodus of the time into the banking industry. I started my banking job at the prestigious Chase Bank on Awolowo Road , Ikoyi. However, one year in the banking industry cured me of my banking dreams for life and indeed of any dead-end 9-5 job.

Still searching for what to do that would catch my passion, I wandered accidentally into furniture and interior design. I got a job at Casafina, and it was there that my passion for furniture was ignited. I spent one year at the company honing my skills and generally preparing myself. After that I left the place to set up DESIGN OPTIONS in 1987 with my friend and colleague, Ifeyinwa Ighodalo , and the rest, as they say, is history.

Ifeyinwa and I clicked right from the beginning. I loved her enthusiasm and drive. In addition, she was focused and had run her parents' interior design business in Enugu before coming to Lagos. We realized that we both had a passion for creative furniture and a good 'eye' for interiors, so relating together on the job became a breeze. We also realized that people believed in us and our ideas, and were willing to trust us with their houses, offices, projects etc. This was the motivation we needed to put our own team of carpenters, upholsters, and handymen together and establish a first rate company.

It is particularly interesting to note that most of the workers we started with twenty years ago are still with us today, ...and we have been very much a part of their lives, their marriages, childbirths, and career paths etc.

It is equally interesting to note that when we started Design Options there were not many young ladies who had our looks and poise:

articulate, confident, stylish, and doing what we were doing. I personally encountered numerous problems with men who thought they were entitled to more than the furniture they were paying for.

However, I found the following helpful to get over that; firstly, the fact that I was married helped a lot, as people still respected the institution of marriage in those days, in the 90's. Secondly, having an exposed and confident spouse who was financially stable, and who shared my passion and respected my talent was another saving grace. And finally, I had a vision and a clearly defined roadmap to getting there, this helped me to know what to do and what not to do.

By this time I was also raising three very active boys at home. As a hands-on parent. I had to create a balance between my home-life and my business so that 'the husband' does not start to resent 'the business.' Creating that balance was work in itself. It helped however to have my mother, sisters, and in-laws that I could call on at short notice for assistance, especially when I needed to travel for international fairs and exhibitions.

Growing up under a very strict disciplinarian as a father laid the platform for a life of meticulous planning and detail for me. My father never left anything to chance. My mother, on the contrary, was the opposite. In this regard, I find that I possess my father's strict discipline about money matters, budget, and time-keeping, but not his rigidity when it comes to stubbornly sticking to the script regardless of whose ox is gored in the process.

I like my mum's playfulness and her "whatever-may-be" approach to life. She is happy and content; always looking at the bigger and brighter picture; very accommodating and easy to get along with. I hope I have imbibed all of these qualities as well.

It was my mum who taught me the fear of God, regardless of who is watching or not. She also taught me to be honest and truthful regardless of personal loss or gain, be it to a friend or foe. I always bring that to play in my business. Clients are amazed when I refund money to them because I had erroneously overcharged them and they were not even aware. My customers appreciate that I tell them the truth regardless of whether it will cost me the sale or not, and even when it is obvious that they caused the error due to their own stubbornness. I am still willing to correct it at any cost because a good interior speaks more than a thousand words or explanation.

I would say my business really took off in the late 1990's-cum-early 2000. Nigerians began to appreciate the benefit of coming home (and going to work) in a beautiful, well-laid out and enabling environment. Everything they were travelling abroad to buy could now be manufactured locally. Moreover, people's taste (and income) had improved because of more international exposure, they were now ready to commit their money to 'tried and trusted' hands to take the stress off them. In fact the dynamics of the whole economy was changing and becoming more international in orientation.

Having said that much about growth, I must also mention that the government really did nothing to encourage the private sector and aspiring young Nigerian entrepreneurs. The necessary infrastructures were lacking, policies to strengthen the private small and medium scale enterprises were non-existent. Strategically, government did not provide leadership or guidance to financial institutions to support growth. So we were really on our own to fathom a way out of the 'hell-hole'. The fact that we have succeeded is a testament to the strength of the organised private sector that continues to contribute to the growth of the Nigerian economy.

In my twenty years in business, the question I get asked often is 'the secret' behind my successful 20 years partnership with Ifeyinwa'. The answer is so simple, it is TRUST. Do we have cat fights…? Yes! We surely do, especially more so as we get older and are more set in our ways. But the truth is that we love each other dearly and value our friendship and the individuality that each person brings to the table that creates that unique blend of our company. Furthermore, we would go the extra mile of bringing in a third party that we both respect and admire (if we reach a deadlock) for conflict resolution.

The truth is that conflict will always arise where two people are involved. My advice is to agree to a blueprint for conflict resolution when entering any partnership, and go along with someone you like, who shares your passion, drive, enthusiasm. Go with your gut feeling and don't be afraid to try.

One of my most memorable experiences in my running of our factory was about ten years ago, when my staff decided to down tools and declared a strike!

I had seen it coming, as I had already noticed some "deadbeat employees" in our recent employment. Deadbeat employees rub their negativity and pessimism on others, they are forever criticizing, complaining and carrying rumours. I regret not nipping them in the bud earlier and firing them immediately. As it turned out, I called out my workshop floor manager and foreman (whom I had started out with from the scratch) and told them in no uncertain terms that I would shut down the factory, sack them all and return to gardening if they think they could hold me to ransom. Then I entered my car and drove away, telling them to call me from my comfortable house when they were ready to work. That ended the mutiny. I stood my ground and called their bluff despite the huge outstanding deliveries we had at hand. And that was the end of that forever...I pray!

I realised that day that indecision was no strength where workers are concerned; the "meaner" you are the more respect you get, being nice is regarded as a weakness, especially in a male-dominated environment like ours.

Another experience I will never forget that had a more profound effect on me happened one day when a client I admired, from the pages of newspaper, called me to furnish his country home. This was a "big" man, by anybody's standard, with huge interests in oil, banking, telecom, manufacturing etc. The work was at the finishing stages when I called him to discuss outstanding sums, and I was asked to see him in his office.

I was sitting across the desk from him when, lo and behold, he suddenly leapt across his desk and lunged at me trying to grab or kiss or whatever, to my utmost surprise and embarrassment. In shock and bewilderment, I shouted at him, "Chairman! Sir...what is the meaning of this?

I was shaking like a leaf and I demanded an apology, which he refused to tender. So I walked out of his office. To this day I cannot reconcile that indecent act with the person I thought of as a respectable citizen with so many titles, including the CON (Commander of the Order of the Niger). I never told my husband because I secretly blamed myself for being so naïve. But I learnt an invaluable lesson that day: NEVER MEET A MALE CLIENT ALONE (even in his office) and NEVER JUDGE A BOOK BY ITS COVER, or by your own standards.

Five years ago, I woke up one day and realised that I had been so busy developing the 'Design Option' brand and raising a family, and had totally forgotten about ME. I took stock of my life and realised that there was no ME in my agenda for self-development, no time to exhale or even spread my wings and explore other talents and dreams. I figured it was time for ME to "get my groove back!"

That year I enrolled into the Lagos Business School and joined the Owners Managers Programme (OMP 2) sceptical that I would never find the time to attend and complete the course. It was an eye-opener for me, being in a class with successful owner managers from various backgrounds, sharing ideas and learning from seasoned professionals. For the first time in ten years, I was in a classroom putting formulas to processes I had been running for years, processes that needed definition and fine-tuning.

This experience encouraged me to apply to another business school in Barcelona , Spain for a programme organised by the LBS. but I was so disappointed about the way my enrolment was handled that I got there and demanded for a full refund of my money.

However, regardless of the challenges we had faced and are still facing in business, we have managed to remain at the forefront of the interior decorating business. We have also worked harder this year, more than ever before, on strengthening our No 1 position in the marketplace by fine-tuning our processes and procedures, so as to leave a lasting legacy to the new generation of professional architects, decorators, and other artisans to take this company to greater heights.

KOFO AKINKUGBE

7

Name:
KOFO AKINKUGBE
(NEE SHONUBI)

Name of Company:
INTERFACE TECHNOLOGIES
SECURE ID

Post:
MANAGING DIRECTOR

Industry:
E-PAYMENT, TELECOMS & E-
IDENTIFICATION SECTORS

BACKGROUND

I grew up in a large family of 10 children. Education was a vital point in our upbringing, which made my siblings and I grow up to be quite studious and determined for academic success. As a timid yet ambitious child, I found it somehow difficult to express my dreams and aspirations to people. So I carried along in life with a lot of passion and ideas hidden inside me.

Thanks to my upbringing, I learnt very early in life that God was my source and my true friend. So it was quite easy for me to place my trust in Him. And I must say that He has never failed, as I have seen the results of trusting HIM every step of the way. And this has caused my confidence to grow and led me to the conclusion that there is no height I cannot attain.

When I look in retrospect, I discovered that I have not been someone who joins the bandwagon. On the contrary, I have always found myself doing the 'not so popular'. For instance, this can be seen in my choice to study Mathematics at the university, or my choosing to operate in an industry that is ostensibly male dominated, among other similar choices I had made.

I am a graduate of Mathematics. And after my Youth Service Corps, I started my working career in the banking industry, where I remained for over 12 years until I left to start Interface Technologies, a security management and biometrics technologies company.

My leaving the banking industry was a major step towards pursuing my gut feeling that 'there is more out there'. While in the bank, I had taken one year break to do an MBA programme. But upon my return to the bank I suddenly felt dissatisfied with the system and work became a mere routine to me. I therefore consider it unfair on the bank for me to continue working there, as I felt I was no longer adding any value. So I decided to resign in order to search for my passion.

Adding to my restlessness then was the fact that I found the banking industry to be focused more on the domestic market at that time (of course this has changed now) and I so badly wanted to operate in the global market. It is important to mention that I left banking at a time when my career was upwardly promising in 1997. And I could have easily risen through the ranks to top management. But I decided to leave all the same and was without a job and pay for three months.

But, during that period, I went all out to seek information, mentors, networking and possible areas of interests that would appeal to my interest. I really had no plan to become an entrepreneur and basically had an open mind to whatever direction God was going to lead me.

After three months of soul-searching and research, an idea came to me to go into biometrics technology, which was an untapped sector in the country then. I then set up Interface Technologies Ltd. (ITL) and ran it for nine years. It was a period of fun and many achievements which culminated in the birth of SecureID Nigeria Ltd., an offshoot from a small department in Interface Technologies. Having run Interface Technologies on an entrepreneurial level, my dream was to establish a structured organisation that will operate in the international global market. ITL had a cards unit which today is now a cards manufacturing/personalization company, SecureID.

I had a dream to set up a world class Smartcard plant that can operate internationally. During the setting up process, the first thing I did was to draw up a business plan. And with the help of a business consultant, I drew up a roadmap/timeline that would serve as my guide to attaining predetermined milestones as well as measure my progress in the process.

Because of the high capital outlay requirement of my project, I approached individuals whom I felt would not only invest their funds, but would also add value towards the success of the company. And the choices of these individuals were prayerfully and carefully made.

It was clear to me where SecureID was heading. I had a mental picture of this dream all the time. I wanted it to be a world-class concern in the global smartcard market. To achieve this end, it was ideal for us to be certified by the VISA International or

Mastercard. So we immediately set out to apply for the VISA certification, and against all odds we got the certification! Today, to the glory of God, after just two years in operation, we are the first VISA certified plant in sub-Saharan Africa!

Of course there were many challenges; a vision goes through an incubation period before birth. My first challenge was combining my roles as a wife and a mother with going after my business goals. I also had to deal with different issues in the business world that I hadn't even imagined before. There were many negative voices and very difficult circumstances that seemed insurmountable. But despite all we got our certification in record time.

Some of the negative and discouraging things I was told were:
- It could take two years to get a VISA certification!
- You cannot get it on the first review!
- You need X amount of money to get the company ready for certification!
- Nigeria is high risk, there are high level of frauds, poor press etc

Being a strong believer in the role of a woman both

in the home and towards her husband, I try to carry my spouse along at every stage of my business. I am first his wife before the entrepreneur. My husband is a director of SecureID and he has been greatly supportive towards the success of the company. He gives invaluable advice to me. And he is someone I regularly bounce off ideas on.

I believe the blessing and support of a spouse is important for entrepreneurial success. Peace in the home gives you a clear vision and makes it a lot easier for you to take logical and correct decisions. A home without peace could delay the actualization of your dream/vision as a woman. Also it is good to have someone that will always tell you the bitter truth when you are going off-track. My simple advice to every woman who wants to pursue entrepreneurship is that chasing your dreams should not be at the neglect of your spouse.

My business role model is Mrs. Ibukun Awosika. I simply admire her strong entrepreneurial skills and her passion for and generosity to the works of the Lord. I find the fact that she is a woman, with a husband and children just like me, coupled with so many achievements behind her tail, quite endearing.

My value system is benchmarked on the word of God. Whatever I am doing, I always ask myself, "Will it please God?" "Is my management style pleasing to Him?" I am also a stickler for a high level of professional conducts in business. To me professionalism is very important.

The effect of my value system on my business has been the success we have today. I have learnt a long time ago that when God is your Source, the success you experience will be far greater than the success that comes from human efforts, hard work etc. And I would rather have that than what my intelligence and efforts could fetch me.

Growth challenges will always exist in any business. They could be with people, or building the right team. We have our fair share of them, but as they come, God has been helping us to overcome them and forge ahead. My dream is still ongoing. I cannot say that I am there yet. I still have a lot more to learn and to achieve.

My exit strategy is to build a legacy of a business that will attract the best managers worldwide who will take over from me one day, continue from where I stop, and move the company to greater heights.

At the end of my days, I would like to be remembered for making a positive impact in people's lives!

NGOZI NZEGWU

8

Name:
NGOZI NZEGWU
(NEE OKWODU)

Name of Company:
DUGO LIMITED

Post:
MANAGING DIRECTOR

Industry:
CUSTOMIZED PRINTING, GIFTS,
AWARDS, AND KEEPSAKES

BACKGROUND

I was born into a very close knit Christian family. My parents are educationists. My father is an economist graduate from London School of Economics, while my mother is a trained teacher. Both of them are now retired.

My parents are also disciplinarians, so I learnt quite early in life that there is no shortcut to hard work. The discipline and strong Christian upbringing I had helped to give me stability and focus throughout my student years. Each time I had to go back to school after a holiday, the last word with which my father always ended his exhortation to me was "Remember whose child you are and whose name you bear in everything you do."

I have a BSc in Sociology as my first degree from University of Lagos. I also went back there for an MBA programme shortly thereafter. In addition, I had the privilege of attending various training programs both at middle and senior management level when I started working.

I started my working experience in the banking industry, which I believe remains one of the most disciplined and rigorous environment anyone can work. And because I always like to excel in everything I do, I gained an in-depth core banking experience in the process and moved up the corporate ladder quite rapidly. But when the stress was becoming too much I decided to resign.

Although I resigned at a senior management level, I never had any exit strategy whatsoever. Neither did I have any significant savings that I could use to start a business. Nevertheless, I was very sure of one thing: I wanted to be my own Boss!

I believe the inspiration that led to my venturing out on my own came from God, coupled with my desire to be my own boss. I have always wanted to do something creative and add value. So after quitting my banking job, I wanted to run a business that revolves around my passion. I believe there are so many things in life that will catch your eyes, but only very few will capture your heart; and that is your passion!

My personal mission for business, which eventually became a corporate mission, is "to create a visual message that will complement my clients' sentiment with unique products and services." I want my business to consistently represent quality, with refined elegance. Today the Dugo brand has become a world class leader in the provision of customized and creative solution to business promotion, awards, recognition and timeless keepsakes using state of the art technology while ensuring extra-ordinary quality at all times.

For every business, information is important. So in order to achieve this vision I started reading books, magazines, and also attended trade shows, seminars, conferences - both locally and abroad - in customized printing, recognition products/programs, and business promotion.

It is important to note that at this time I did not have money, but the vision was so captivating that I just could not stop. At the back of my mind were always these three key words: - 'the concept,' 'the product,' 'the process.' And an exclamation from a satisfied customer that "Is this done in Nigeria?"

After I zeroed in on my plan to start a custom imprinting business, I approached my bank with my proposal. As a banker it was easy to package the facility. And based on the confidence my bank had in me, the credit was approved.

The first challenge I encountered in the course of achieving my vision was the fear of the unknown. I dreaded the possibilities of what could happen as a result of my stepping out of my comfort zone, as a comfortable banker, for the uncertainties-ridden world of entrepreneurship.

Secondly, I resigned without any significant savings and so did not really have any chunk capital to start the business. Finally, I was so consumed with my banking career that I did not have an exit strategy as to what to do after I quit. So it took me a while to articulate the type of business I wanted to do.

I prayed fervently and had peace within me that God wanted me to leave my career, and that gave me a lot of confidence. Moreover, I have always believed that the best way to predict the future is to create it. So I decided to take the plunge anyway.

My greatest challenge came when I borrowed some very short-term funds to purchase equipment, and before I could start using the machine the loan was due for payment! What happened was that the equipment arrived during a strike by clearing agents, so I did not take delivery of it on time to start work. And when I eventually did, the loan was near redemption!

So I went to my bank and explained my predicament to them, and after a long period of pressure they agreed to restructure the facility for me. But I ended up paying four times more than what was borrowed!

I learnt a very big lesson from this experience; that is never to use short-term funds to finance the purchase of fixed assets. Another big challenge I had to contend with, which has to do with my industry, was meeting production deadline at short notice. Overcoming this hurdle has forced us to increase our in-house capacity for custom imprinting in the process. This means that we also control the quality and craftsmanship of our works every step of the way.

What I could term as our greatest challenge so far was the ban on the importation of some of the products we offer by the federal government of Nigeria. This has however made us looked inward, and presently we are working on manufacturing some of our products locally. In a nutshell, the challenges we face are actually making us go full circle to serve our customers better, as we believe where there is willingness, great challenges become small!

My husband has always been a tower of support for me spiritually, morally and financially, and this has helped me greatly in the fulfillment of my vision and dream. I doubt if I would have dared to pursue my vision without his support. As a professional himself, he is highly secured and has a lot of confidence in my entrepreneurial ability.

God created a woman to be a helper to a man. Therefore, right from creation a woman derives her identity first from God and secondly from her husband. I strongly believe that a woman's performance is at its peak when she has the support of her husband. As a female entrepreneur, if you have a spouse who is not threatened by your success; the sky is just the beginning and not the limit.

My parents taught me to be very confident in myself and to dare to soar in anything. Growing up in a family where there is so much bond of love reinforces that confidence, coupled with the ingrained Christian teaching that with God nothing is impossible. We are all excited and concerned about each other's accomplishments in my family. And this is a vital support system that I regularly recourse to.

I do not have a specific role model in business. But I admire people like Hillary Clinton, Oprah Winfrey, Martha Stewart, Jack Welch, Aliko Dangote, and Gbolade Osibodu for their fighting spirit, their staying power and creation of wealth.
The core values that I hold dearly are: integrity, excellence, and quality. And these are my submissions on them:

A. Integrity: the highest courage is to be yourself in the face of adversity. Choosing right over wrong, ethics over convenience, and truth over popularity. There is never a wrong time to do the right thing.

B.   Quality: the race for quality has no finish line.

C.   Excellence: is never an accident. It is always, the result of high intention, sincere effort, intelligent direction, skillful execution and the vision to see obstacles as opportunities. Those who attain excellence commonly spend life in a focused pursuit. I have learnt that on the road to success there is never a crowd on the extra mile!!

We live in an environment where values are upside down. For me, it's a daily challenge, determination and, above all, the grace of God to fight and ensure that my fundamental values are not rubbished or compromised. In the long run, it always pays off to stand your ground and fight for your values.
Even after the business has already found its footing, I still faced the following growth challenges of:

1.   Getting the crop of staff who shares my passion and vision.

2. Increasing overheads due to poor infrastructure, especially the cost of power generation.

3. Getting the banks to see the potentials that exist in my business so as to give timely financial support.

My exit/handing over strategy? Wow! I'm still trying to figure it out. I am working on getting external investors, and I am putting in place a succession structure.

At the end of my days, I want to be remembered as someone who died empty, having completed 100% of my assignment.

Beyond running a successful conglomerate, I want to take about 2000 young Nigerians off the unemployment lists in the next 10 years. I want to increasingly invest a substantial part of our profit into the empowerment of Christian business women, through the provision of micro-credit facilities and capacity-building in my Kingdom Investors Ministry. I also intend to raise partners to support this ministry, and I want to invest more time and resources in NGOs and Ministries that I am involved with.

For me success is not an end but a means to an end, and that end is the ultimate purpose for which God created me. I want to leave a legacy of what has eternal value!!

Finally, I want to be remembered as a virtuous woman; a devoted wife and mother to my husband and children respectively.

MUNI SHONIBARE

9

Name:
MUNI SHONIBARE
(NEE ATTA)

Name of Company:
ETHNIKI LTD
INTERIOR OPTIONS LTD

Post:
MANAGING DIRECTOR

Industry:
FURNITURE

BACKGROUND

I was born as Muni Atta. I am the oldest in a family of eight children. I married Supo Shonibare just before my 30th birthday.

By then I had already graduated from the Instituto Per Arte Restauro, Florence, Italy. There I gained valuable exposure and experiences which also helped me considerably in life as well as enhanced my performance while working as a resident interior designer for a Kaduna based architectural firm; Habibat Associates. Later on I resigned from there and co-founded Avant Grade, a company that specialized in developing interior design schemes for residences, offices and hospitality outfits in Kaduna and Lagos.

My father was a diplomat, so we traveled extensively and were exposed to very diverse peoples and cultures across 4 continents. These created a keen awareness of the uniqueness of every individual in my mind, and as a result I grew up to respect other people's rights to individuality, religions, norms and cultures.

My appreciation and love of creative arts, such as music, literature, art, etc., plus a compulsive need on my part to add aesthetic value to my life and the lives of others helped me to arrive at the vision that led to the birth of Interior Options which I founded in 1987.

It has grown from an interior design and furniture showroom in Kaduna to a large furniture factory with offices and showrooms in Lagos and Abuja, employing over one hundred Nigerian staff with a sprinkling of expatriates.

The first job of Interior Options was the renovation of my father's house which proved to be a great advertisement for the company and led to many referrals. A popular saying is "seeing is believing." And that is certainly the case of our products; they sold themselves!

Did I face some challenges in building my business? The answer is a Big Yes! As a young and naïve lady, I was faced with tough moments dealing with some difficult situations. Lack of skilled and committed staff with the right attitude to share my vision and passion, coupled with lack of essential infrastructures are some of the greatest challenges that I faced in the course of achieving my set goals.

I have been able to overcome challenges with a sense of direction, focus, discipline and commitment, and my business goals are gradually being realized. It is constant work in progress though.

I strongly believe a partner's confidence in and support of a female entrepreneur is crucial toward the actualization of her entrepreneurial dream.

My husband played a very committed, supportive and encouraging role in my business. His implicit belief in my capabilities is one of the motivating factors that goad me to aim as high as I can. Whenever occasion demands, he has no reservations about rising up to take over family functions that are traditionally my responsibility.

My family members have been my greatest supporters and advertisers in whatever I do. I consider myself truly privileged to be a part of the family I find myself in.

The values that I treasure the most and which have added to the success I have accomplished in business are integrity, quality, innovativeness, sincerity, creativity, discipline and commitment. These value systems have helped in establishing the goals of Interior options, from the initial stage and have also differentiated us from the rest.

As I move the company to the next level, I am putting structures and systems in place. I also plan to organize series of training programmes for staff to identify individuals with the right qualities; that is people that share the passion and vision of the company, so that together we can join forces to build a world-class company.

When I have done my bit and my time is over, I would like to be remembered as someone with integrity, sincerity of purpose and an innovative leader of design furniture manufacturing. In addition, I hope I am remembered as an inspiration to women to find their voice and themselves.

OYINADE AJE

10

Name:
OYINADE AJE
(NEE SOKOYA)

Name of Company:
SATIN & LACE

Post:
MANAGING DIRECTOR

Industry:
FASHION & STYLES

BACKGROUND

My name is Oyinade Aje. I am the second child in a family of six children. Growing up was a bit unsettling but great fun as we travelled from country to country and changed schools numerous times due to my father's job. This afforded me the opportunity of interacting with people of diverse races. In short, my early days exposed me to different cultures which obviously impacted my life significantly and helped in shaping who I turned out to be today.

My dream as a child was to be different. I wanted to try my hands at something a lot of people hadn't tried their hands on. I always dreamt of doing something novel and exciting with my life, like being a model or a beautician, which when I was growing up would have been different in Nigeria.

When I finished my Youth Corps service, I worked as a solicitor with a law firm, Phillip & Begho & Co., at Western House. Later I moved to NGM where I worked as the Legal Adviser/Company Secretary for some time, before I was transferred to take up the Acting General Manager position of a travel Agency owned by the group.

I remember that when I was younger, I always said "By the time I am 30 years old, I'll have my own business." I have always known that I wasn't cut out for the 9-5 work routine. I knew I had to do my own thing, my own way. You could say I discovered myself quite early. I have always been creative and I have always longed to use my hands, and I have been doing so for 20 years now... Wow! How time flies!

One day, a lady in my church asked me to help her make a tiara for her renewal of vows to her husband. Now, I had never done such a thing before. But never being the one to say "I can't" I agreed to do it. So armed with a bridal magazine and some rather crude tools, I managed to make something quite beautiful. On the day of the ceremony another friend whispered in my ears, "Oyinade, if you don't commercialize this talent God will be cross with you o." That was my "aha" moment, as Oprah would say. The light bulb just came on and I decided right there and then that I would start making handcrafted bridal accessories!

Having made the all important decisions as to the type of business to venture into, I travelled abroad, first to Hong Kong and then to London where I stayed for two years and soaked in all that the creative atmosphere London had to offer. I also bought books and borrowed some from various libraries in a bid to educate and equip myself, as I found out that it wasn't easy to get the formal training I needed for the business

London is a very creative place and if you already have creativity in you, just being there is an inspiration also. I have an innate gift that when I take a look at something I can pretty much figure out how it was made. While in London, I also bought all the tools and materials that I would need to start the business. Then I came back to Nigeria and started Satin & Lace in 1991.

The challenges you face in business are different as the business is changing and growing. When I first started, being a pioneer company, the challenge was gaining credibility and acceptance, and getting people to believe in you and what you are doing. One of the things that motivated me to start the business was the desire to let people know both in Nigeria and abroad that beautiful things can come out of this blessed country of ours, and you don't have to go across the shores for all things beautiful.

With growth, the challenge is ensuring that the core values of the business are not eroded or compromised; by recruiting the right staff and paying attention to other associated HR issues, as well as ensuring that proper structure and processes are put in place. In Nigeria, we have a very unique workforce, and it takes nothing but the grace of God to employ and retain the right crop of workers to accompany you on your journey.

Of course growing a business requires capital and that too can be challenging. Raising capital for a small business owner is fraught with all sorts of difficulties that can be discouraging. For me as a creative entrepreneur, I would really rather concentrate on the creative side of things and not bother myself with the day-to-day management of the company; checking accounts and inventory etc. I feel I need my thinking space so I can create, create and innovate. However, reality demands that I must pay attention to that side of the business as well, if I don't want a mess on my hands at the end of the day.

In the early days my husband wasn't that involved in the business. But he didn't in any way curtail me. He gave me the liberty to pursue my dream; the only condition he gave was that my commitment to the family should not suffer consistently because of the business, and that I try my best to comply with. Now that the business is growing he has become more involved and supportive, as he does not want me to buckle up under the pressure.

A spouse is truly very important in the fulfilment of the entrepreneurial dream. On your own you can achieve, especially if God is with you, but having the support and encouragement of an understanding spouse makes the entire entrepreneurial journey much easier and fulfilling. To have someone by you to hold your hand when the going gets tough, as it inevitably does, is a resource not to be underestimated, but one to constantly celebrate. The way I see it, business is tough enough, particularly in our environment, without you having to encounter hostility from your partner at the home front. That will surely have a destabilizing effect on any woman.

Family is important as well in achieving the entrepreneurial end, especially if they have bought into your dream and vision. What premium could you possibly place on the value of a family member who encourages you, makes money and collateral available for you when the chips are down? It is simply unquantifiable.

My business role models are Mrs. Ibukun Awosika, Mrs. Nike Ogunlesi, and Mr. Leke Alder. They are a constant source of inspiration to me personally and to many others in business. I applaud their achievements and contributions to present day Nigeria.

As for my value system, I believe in honesty and fair play. For me you must always strive for a win-win situation in business. I believe very strongly in excellence. After all, I have the excellent spirit of God within me. Therefore, I believe whatever you are doing in life, no matter how mundane you may think it is, adding the touch of excellence to it will make a world of difference. As Bishop Mike Okonkwo once said, "even if you are selling groundnut, do it with excellence!" As children of God when we do things excellently well, we honour God, we show the world the children of whom we are, and bring glory to our heavenly Father.

One area my value system has helped me to achieve success is that when people know who you are and what you stand for; they will readily do business with you and keep coming back. And that has been our story at Satin & Lace. When we first started business, not a lot of people knew about us. But whenever they saw our work they assumed it was imported, and upon realizing that it was made in Nigeria they were always bowled over.

That is what a value system of excellence does for you. The Bible says, 'See a man diligent in his work, he will stand before kings and queens and not before mere men' (Proverbs 22:29). I make bold to surmise that the word "diligent" as this Bible verse puts it is not just about working hard. No, it is more that that. It is about working hard, working well, and working excellently. Excellence attracts. I believe the only way the works of our hands can praise us at the city gates is when they are excellently executed.

IBUKUN AWOSIKA

11

Name:
IBUKUN AWOSIKA
(NEE ADEKOLA)

Name of Companies:
THE CHAIR CENTRE
SOKOA CHAIR CENTRE
FURNITURE MANUFACTURERS' MART

Post:
MANAGING DIRECTOR

Industry:
FURNITURE

BACKGROUND

I was born on the 24th of December 1962 to the Adekola family as Bilkisu Abiodun Motunrayo Omobolanle Ibidunni. I am the third child in a Moslem family then of seven children. My family has a strong Islamic heritage, as my father's maternal grandfather was the first Alhaji in the city of Ibadan, in the days when they used to ride on camels to Mecca. I was born to a Nigerian father, Mr Abdulmashood Adekola of Oke-Foko Ibadan, and a Cameroonian mother, Hannah Aduke Adekola nee Ashu of Tinto village in Western Cameroon.

Most of my early years were spent with my grandmother, as I was left with her when I was about a year old while my parents went to England to further their education. I believe my first exposure to business in any form was sitting at my grandmother's little shop where she sold salt. I enjoyed a lot of care and affection in my early days, the type that one could get from a grandmother who was not sure if her son who had gone to a far away land would ever come back to her. That was the mind-set then.

I remember when my parents felt my brother and I would be spoilt by my grandmother, they told her to send us to a nursery boarding school. This helped me to build an independent mindset right from my early years. Whenever my grandmother came visiting my brother and I in the school, she would hide food under her "iborun" (shoulder drapes) because she was convinced that we were not well fed. She would tell us to quickly eat the food with tears in her eyes expressing the love of a grandmother who felt she was being forced to give her grandchildren away. But my parents were convinced that growing up in the family house was not the best for us.

Some years later, my parents returned with my siblings; and my father's first job was at UAC farms in Minna, Niger state. We spent some time there before we moved back to Lagos. This meant that my primary school education was in different places. But the most interesting part was that I completed my primary education in a public school, St. Paul African Church Primary School in

Lagos, while my other siblings all went to private schools.

From there I proceeded to Methodist Girls High School (popularly called MG) for my secondary school education. This I consider a critical part of my life, because from form two I got involved in a lot of activities in school such as sports, debate, choir etc because I was so restless. Nevertheless, I was still outstanding in my academic performance as well, and though I was a Moslem then, I read the valedictory message for my set in church.

In the school then, a lot of girls from Moslem families did not like being called by their Moslem names because the names sound like the names of their housemaids at home. But I was insistent on being called Bilkisu, as I was very proud of my Islamic heritage and self assured enough not to be embarrassed by my name as some were.

I thoroughly enjoyed my secondary school days and made a lot of friends there, some of which have lasted till date. Some of my friends and classmates from then include Gbolahan Babalakin (nee Jinadu) and her sister Dupe Jinadu (of blessed memory, who was my best friend and sister then, but died while we were writing our school certificate exams). Others are Kemi Onasogun, Subu Giwa-Amu, Sade Ladenegan, Kike Longe, and Dupe Kazeem.

I particularly remember with great respect our principal then, Mrs Onafowokan, who was indeed a mother, a source of encouragement, and a disciplinarian that tolerated no nonsense from anyone. Whenever I think about my days at MG, I am always grateful to God for going to a school with values and one which helped to build a good foundation of multi-tasking and a sense of adventure, to try one's hands on different things at the same time, in me.

As I was preparing for the university, I initially wanted to become a medical doctor. However, I found out from a friend's brother who was a medical student that they actually use real human corpses for some of their experiments. This made me abandon the idea. I could not cut a fly; much less a human body, dead or alive. I then aspired to work as an architect because I loved drawing and designing. Although I was a science student, I really loved Fine Art.

I sat and passed my JAMB exams for admission into the University of Ife (now Obafemi Awolowo University). But the results of our Physics papers at the O' level for my school was delayed. And when it was eventually released a few months later, though I got an "A" in physics, it was too late to meet my admission. So I had to retake the JAMB exams again, but this time I was admitted into Chemistry department.

I must point out here that if I had been exposed to some counselling and career advice, I wouldn't have found myself where I did. Even though I was in the science class and passed all my science subjects very well, yet my personality does not match the sciences. And this is what often happens to the brilliant students who usually get boxed into the science class. If I had gone for any of the social science or business-related courses, perhaps I would have really enjoyed my university days. But as it turned out, I found myself wanting to change my course at Ife, as I really did not enjoy the process of my chemistry degree.

Although I had a good background of excellent academic performance, as I finished with a Grade 1 at Methodist Girls and even won the Dotun Okubanjo prize for the most outstanding student, I got the shocker of my life when I failed a course in my first year at the university. I couldn't reconcile what went wrong. So I decided to change course in my second year. I wanted to change to Law, so I went to the office of the Dean of the Law faculty. After waiting for many hours without giving up, he finally agreed to see me. He turned out to be an elderly professor and wondered what this young lady he had never seen before wanted that made her wait endlessly for him.

I just blurted out "I want to change to Law."

The man looked at me for some time, smiled and finally said, "You know what? I like your courage. If I'm going to take anybody from another department into Law next session, it will be you!"

He however gave me a condition that I must pass very well in my departmental courses before he could take me in for Law. This put me in a dilemma really because if I pass well, my department would not want to release me, and Law would not take me in if I didn't do well.

At the end of that session, I didn't want to study Law anymore. And at a time, I became so confused about it all, and later resolved to become an accountant. So I began to take electives in Accountancy and Administration to complete my units and to prepare myself for a career as an accountant. Funny enough, I performed much better in these elective courses than in my departmental courses. I therefore took all my electives in accountancy till I graduated from the university.

A part of my life which I know contributed in no small measure to the life of business which I chose later was my membership of Junior Chambers International (Jaycees). I had joined the organisation at eighteen and was positively engaged in leadership development and inspiring experiences with the Junior Chambers throughout my years in the university.

Through Jaycees conferences around the world I had visited countries like Korea, Taiwan, Colombia and Canada before I left the university. At those conferences I had seen many outstanding young people from all over the world received awards for the most extra-ordinary achievements through the Outstanding Young Person's Award programme of Jaycees. I had sat under the inspiring talk of men like Edward Heath amongst many others. All of which helped to inspire me to excellence and a desire to be outstanding in whatever I choose to do.

By the age of twenty, I was the president of the University of Ife chapter managing over one hundred members, both younger and older than I was. I believe this greatly prepared me for the management of my staff all of whom were men, who were much older than I was in the early years of the business, and to interact confidently with different cadre of people who were my possible customers as the business grew.

After graduation, I naturally proceeded for my NYSC which was in Kano state. I know people don't really think much about the NYSC scheme. But I will like to point out here that the programme adds significant value. There are people from different parts of the country that I wouldn't have met or have as friends today if not for the NYSC. Moreover, the paramilitary exercises, such as the morning jogging, endurance trek etc have their own values too. I agree that the scheme needs a lot of restructuring, but it is a laudable initiative. Besides, it offers majority of our graduates their first job experience.

I was initially sent to a school to teach chemistry as my primary assignment. But I didn't want to teach. Rather, I wanted to use my service year to prepare for a career as an accountant by taking ICAN exams. So I went to report at the school where I was deployed. Knowing full well that it was a fundamental Islamic school, I went there with an open-necked dress in order to discourage them from taking me. My plan worked. One look at me and the principal promptly rejected me.

I then returned to the NYSC zonal office and asked to be posted to an accounting firm. The zonal officer did not agree at first, but when I sat at the front of the office of the panel in charge of posting for three days from morning till evening, they finally decided to send me to the Kano office of Akintola Williams & Co. which was what I wanted all along.

I am grateful for that one year of service at Akintola Williams, because it afforded me the needed exposure to relevant books on accounting as well as field experience. I also learned the value of book-keeping in the process. But sadly enough, at the end of the day I realised that I did not want to work as an accountant anymore. From the way I saw it then, the life of an auditor does not allow much room for creativity and use of initiative. Certain laid down procedures must be followed, and deviating from this norm will be considered as insubordination. Even though I had started the ICAN exams, I packed up and returned to Lagos at the end of my service year with the intention of getting a job in a bank.

However, I did not want to sit at home doing nothing while awaiting the banking job, I wanted any job. During my NYSC, I got myself occupied by presenting a programme on CTV Kano, doing voice over for TV commercials, and I also drew on my athletic knowledge in my secondary school and university days to conduct aerobic classes. All of these were other streams of income for me, and made me quite financially independent during my service year.

The first job I could get whilst waiting for the bank job was at a furniture company. I had gone to see Fola Adeola, one of my adopted big brothers, who gave me a note to the MD of the furniture company. And after being interviewed I was offered a job at the Ikoyi showroom of the company.

I am grateful to Fola Adeola for being the vessel through whom God used to set me on the path to destiny. I didn't know about the company or the furniture business then, neither did I have any desire to start a furniture manufacturing business. But that singular act of sending me to the furniture company, which was the biggest and most successful furniture company around then, was a destiny-definer for me.

As it turned out, I only lasted three and a half months there. But during this period I discovered that I thoroughly enjoyed the process of changing space by using furniture and its accessories. I also derived so much pleasure in advising and counselling people on how to go about it. But I had strong reservations about certain things in the company where I worked.

One day while at work, a gentleman, brother of a friend of mine who was an architect walked into the showroom to make enquiry about some furniture he needed for a project he was working on. Later, we sat together to talk and I shared with him my dream to start a furniture manufacturing business of my own with a different structure and values. And he said whenever I was ready I should contact him, as he was interested.

Eventually when I felt that I had enough and was going to start out on my own, with absolutely no money to start with, I called him and asked if he was still interested in us working as partners. My thinking then was that, he being an architect and I selling furniture, we could create a partnership. He was interested. He told me that he had registered a business whose name I later changed to Quebees Ltd, with his father as the chairman, and he as a director, and that we could start the business using that name, which we did.

The partnership took off with me working in one room in his office at Oyingbo. I hired a carpenter, who in turn helped to hire the other members of the team of seven that I started with. Our first upholstery job was for the family of a friend of my youngest sister. We did the job at the back of our house then at Aguda, using my mother's sewing machine!

Our first big job was for a new bank. I had gone to see Tayo Aderinokun, another adopted big brother of mine, who worked there to ask if there was anything we could do for them. He asked if we could help them to produce paper trays and computer tables. We took up the challenge and decided to work on it. My chief carpenter told me there was an uncompleted building next to where he stayed at Ejigbo. At that time I had never heard of a place called Ejigbo, nor ever been there before, but we needed to do the work and that was the only place available that we knew of, so I really did not mind going there with him. Then he also told me the worst of his fears, that "Molues" were the only means of public transportation to Ejigbo! But that did not deter me as well.

And so we went there and started the job. As at this time, I could not afford to buy any machinery, but in the furniture business the carpenters come with their tools, and that is what I started with. We took our wood processing works to the Sawmills at Amu. I remember that, after completing the job, we took our samples to the Stock Exchange building at Marina. Thank God Tayo saw me first with the samples. He called me aside and said I should take them away quickly before others get to see them. He then encouraged me to go and work on them, assuring me that he knew we could come up with something better. So we went back and worked with all the energy we could muster. Then I took the new samples to Tayo, and he said "now you can present." The bank liked our works and that got us our very first order.

At that time there were a lot of people in the bank who just got new jobs with high pay, or who got promoted to higher ranks. Some of them wanted to refurbish their furniture at home, and because I had developed rapport with them, I got all sorts of job orders. And the fact that it was novelty that a "girl" was the person making the furniture added colour to the process and this also earned me a good number of referrals. As these people moved up the corporate ladder or changed jobs for better ones, I also grew with them. I look back today and I find that my contemporaries are either in top executive positions or heads of some organisations in different sectors of the economy.

From the uncompleted house next to my carpenter's house, we moved to an abandoned building at Papa Ajao. This building belonged to my partner's father, we rented it from him and raised a shed there which we divided into different sections of our operations. We were happy at last to have a place of our own. Gradually we started buying tools from the profit we were making.

At that time Daily Times used to organise a furniture fair, and although we were less than a year, I decided to brave it and told my chief carpenter to put everything we had into the production of what we would be taking for the fair. We worked really hard to present a good front. It was a good experience for me. I realised that we could compete with the big furniture companies in terms of the products on display. And while we sold what we could at the fair, our major take-home was our selection by Texaco (which was building a new office in Lagos) as one of the five companies to bid for the supply of furniture for the new project. Of course they didn't realise that Quebees was run by a young lady in her mid-twenties! Also that we were only six months old as a company!

I worked very hard on our submission with the exuberance and passion which I was sure other companies that were asked to bid wouldn't do. After all, to them it would just be another bidding exercise. I even prepared colourful folders for our presentations.

We were invited and I met a youngish man who could relate to me, so there was no issue about my person yet. We were asked to bring samples, and we worked hard on the chairs and tables we presented. We ended up getting the largest portion of the project. We were then asked to come and sign the contract at the office of the committee's chairman. I remember the amazement in the secretary's face when she saw me. She ushered me into the chairman's office, and he turned out to be an elderly man.

On seeing me, he looked at me briefly and then looked beyond me as if to see the MD of Quebees, whom he supposed I came with and was probably carrying his briefcase. Considering that I was a tall, slim, leggy young woman in short skirt and a shirt, you really cannot blame the man. But when he saw no one behind me, he had to ask me if I was the MD of Quebees, to which I replied in the affirmative. Then he asked again, "Are you sure?" and I gleefully said "Yes," as I was now used to finding myself in such situation.

He hesitantly asked me to sit and asked if I was sure I was capable of executing the job. I assured him that we could, and then I read him our small CV, which was a roll call of our past jobs. He allowed me to sign the contract and said "good luck." He was not very sure we could handle the project satisfactorily. That made me more determined to put my best on the job.

My only challenge at this point was that oil companies do not give down payment. And that was what we used to do most of our works then. So I decided to go seek for a loan to execute the job. But unfortunately, no one was willing to take the risk on an unknown company and an unknown young girl too.

Around that time, Tayo Aderinokun had just started First Marina Trust Ltd. The loan I needed was N50,000 which was a lot of money then in 1989, as the total contract of 58 tables and 58 chairs was N166,000; First Marina, with all the faith Tayo had in me, gave me the money, and I got the break I needed to work hard and deliver on the project.

Unfortunately, the Texaco building was not ready about five months after the stipulated time; whereas the loan we took plus interest was being paid every month. I didn't know what to do. But eventually I decided to write a threatening letter to them that they would have to be paying the interest on our loan. We were therefore invited for a meeting with the project committee and its chairman, Alhaji Danmole, who nicknamed me "baby MD" when he later found out his daughter and I had gone to MG together.

After the meeting, they decided to pay us our money since the fault was not from us. Our ability to deliver the Texaco job boosted our confidence in no small measure, and it also earned us many referrals.

My first major challenge with any job was also on this job, and it tested all my belief that we must keep our word to our customers.

In order to produce the swivel chairs which they ordered, we had searched everywhere for the right swivel base to attach to the upholstered chair seating frame which we produced in our own factory. I eventually decided to buy the bases from a company on Isolo express way owned by some Syrians, mainly because they had given us guaranty on the product. The alternative in the market then were Asian-made ones sold at Idumagbo by guys who will not replace it for you even if it got damaged on the same day that you bought it.

Unfortunately, two weeks after they began using the furniture, the swivel bases started to fall apart. IT WAS A REAL MESS! Within a period of weeks we had 27 out of 58 chairs damaged. This definitely was the worst nightmare of any young company, especially when the base constituted over 50% of the costs of the chair!

I did not think that we had any other choice but to do the right thing by changing all the damaged pieces and keeping our word to the company. Though it was a very painful, expensive and almost destructive experience for us at the point in time, we were able to survive the situation and move forward. I decided not to sell any swivel chairs again until I can sell one that I truly can guaranty.

We went ahead to develop a number of wooden office seats without swivel, and by sharing our past experience with customers, we encouraged them to buy the wooden office seats with four legs, and this we did successfully until some years later when the government lifted the ban on furniture products and we were one of the first to develop and educate the market on the value of a good ergonomic chair through "The Chair Centre", which was born in 1997.

Some years down the line, I was totally dissatisfied for so many reasons: firstly, we could no longer increase our capacity. Secondly, we still did not have the necessary machines to enable us work faster. Jobs kept coming in, but we were not meeting deadlines. We were a young company and not such a force to reckon with by the big companies. There were many job opportunities we couldn't take because we did not have the capacity. And this was really getting to me.

There was a man who worked in an organisation that I had been doing some work for and I also did some jobs for his family. He and his family had taken to me. One fateful day he saw me and asked why I was down, and I told him my many frustrations with the business at that point. Because he had seen the quality of our work, he told me that he was willing to give me a loan of N1 million. But he would only give me the loan through a bank.

So I went to First Marina Trust, and after they had both discussed, I was given the loan, which I had to pay back every 90 days from our profit and would roll over what was left. Unfortunately, the interest rate at that time was very high, 42-70%. But God's mercies gave me good jobs that helped us to meet the obligation. I remember that by the fifteenth month, I got a job that enabled me to pay off the entire loan plus interest, and my final payment was still over N900,000!

But we were happy as we were now able to buy machines and other equipments. We also moved to a much bigger facility. I travelled to England to buy refurbished machineries and this helped to increase our capacity. This was a period when the issue of power supply was most excruciating. We would be in the factory from morning till evening without any power supply. But once we were closing for the day, power would come on. This went on for months on end, and salaries were being paid to workers. It was really frustrating. I really cannot tell how I survived. I just knew that I could not give up. This is the kind of moment when you are grateful that you know God, as it took His grace to keep going.

I saw an advert for the sale of a used 40KV generator on the notice board at Ikoyi club, which I eventually bought through a loan of N120,000 from First Marina Trust Ltd. Thank God for First Marina and their support. Though it was more expensive to use money from a finance house to grow a business, yet the most important thing at that time was that they believed in me enough to continue to give us money any time we needed it.

I can categorically say that for so many years, I kept on ploughing back our profit into the business, and loans were actually additions to our retained profit. By this time people were already calling me "Ijebu" because I had no car, despite the relative success of my business. But a car was not my priority then as I was more concerned about the growing needs of the company. So I was making do with taxis to move from one place to another. A car would mean an immediate expense that I was not willing to make at that time.

While my contemporaries in the banks then were getting loans to buy Daewoo and other posh cars, I knew I had a goal to reach. And the temporary inconvenience was the price I had to pay to meet that goal. Besides, there was no other place I could have gotten the money to buy the car but our profit. This taught me financial discipline. By the time we got to the point where the banks considered us a good business enough to give us loans, we were already making a turnover of N150 million with no debt portfolio, as the ones we collected before were usually short-term, and paid back immediately.

At another stage of the business, having a factory within the compound of The Punch Newspapers at Dopemu was not enough, as most of our customers were on the Island. I had a desire to open a retail store on the Island to reach existing customers, build an increased customer base, and a retail arm for our already made goods. This led me to search for a space in Victoria Island as I was led by the Holy Spirit.

It is important to note that at this time, I was already married and became a Christian shortly before my wedding. And the role of my relationship with God and the wisdom of His word cannot be underplayed in my business decisions as I moved forward. I can also say that it would have been difficult if I didn't have a partner who was there to support me, stand up for and with me through it all. It was like having two MDs in my company, even though he had his own full time work. ABIODUN OLUDOLA AWOSIKA is truly my gift, and God had it all covered when He gave me my own husband.

My family before and after marriage are my support system. I remember when we were still at Papa Ajao, I was still single then and whenever we had to work late my father was the one who usually came to pick me up, while my mother would cook for the 27 men working for me then because there was no food in that area. My sisters, Dupe, Funmi and Dayo were permanently on various assignments for the business, from praying through many projects and trials to running errands anywhere needed.

I didn't know how to deal with local government officials and their many demands, but my dad was always on ground to help me handle that. I also remember one day, after marriage, when my workers tried to blackmail me and made it impossible for us to meet a deadline. I decided to fire everybody; and they in turn locked me up inside the factory. It was my husband that I called, and he came with a friend who was with him at that time. Together they resolved the issues with the workers and I was let out. In fact, I was pregnant with my first child then. I however only took the workers back with fresh applications and on my own terms, after full apologies.

The spouse and family are invaluable support system for any business person, male or female. Biblically, a woman can only do all with godly wisdom and prosper when she has the support and encouragement of her husband. You can win as a woman in all fronts when you have the blessing of God and that of your spouse.

One other support system is your faith, this is because our values and approach to life are guided by our faith system and our home/societal upbringing. Having become a Christian at an early stage of my business, the words I had heard helped me to hold on when many gave up. The truth is, many people also started when I did, and some joined along the way, but many had fallen by the way side. But the grace, mercy, guidance and counsel of God have helped me to move on.

To me, challenges are no more the issue, but getting the solutions. Every major growth in the evolution of my business has been a solution to a challenge, because after every challenging situation, there is always a story. One of my favourite quotes in the Bible is the passage that says, "They that know their God shall be strong and do great exploits" (Daniel 11:32). Therefore, it's the knowing of God, trusting Him, and holding on to Him when nothing seems real that is the distinguishing factor between a success and a failure. With His eyes, I am able to see what is not real and press forward to it. And He does not, and has never failed.

All of this point to the importance of the kind of environment where you choose to worship. No words will fully express my appreciation to Pastors Taiwo and Bimbo Odukoya (of blessed memory) for always being there to stand in prayers with me through all the challenging moments, to give a word, to inspire, and to continually push me to excel in what the Lord has called me to. Truly, The Fountain of Life Church, and the family support system it offers, is an invaluable asset that has contributed in no small measure to what I have become today. It has also given me the boldness to build a successful business institution without compromising or doing it in the general ways of doing business.

Deciding to build a business devoid of corruption, where there will be no bribery, cheating, or helping someone to steal was a tall order for me. But from the start of the business, I had decided that I was not going to sleep with any man to get a business, because how many men can one sleep with in order to get a job, as there will always be finer and more attractive women.

Secondly, I decided that I was not going to pay a bribe to get a business because there will always be someone who can pay higher than what I offer in order to get the same thing. So why bother? Luckily enough, I became a Christian just a year into my business and I started to have understanding of Christianity and the values inherent in the Bible.

I read a book titled God Owns My Business by Tam Stanley. In the book, the author mentions that at a point he decided to make God the majority shareholder of his business with a 51% shareholding, while he and his family held 49%. And bringing God into the business informed the values by which it will be run. I also purposed that I was going to build a business with God at the centre. So I began a search and I came across another book, Business By The Book, by Larry Burkett plus other materials about people who had made God-centred resolutions in the area of business.

Whenever I announced my business values, I was initially told that I was crazy and that it is not possible in Nigeria. Some people think our success was not because we were doing what we said. But God in His own ways usually confirms if this is true or not. The biggest test of our value came when in January 2004 the Nigerian government banned the importation of furniture. Before that time, our business system had developed in a way that we had tooling in different parts of the world and were producing our CKD components outside for assembling in Nigeria, and this was our major line.

But when the ban was announced, for some in the same business it was easier to resort to smuggling as a means of staying in business. But because of whom we are, smuggling was not an option. So I had to seek the face of God for direction on what to do, since I was sure that He would not place my feet on a rock only to remove it beneath me. I was also sure that I am in His will and I'm doing what He wants.

So when everyone around me panicked, I sought the face of God. And He reminded me of a question He had asked me three years earlier that if furniture were banned in Nigeria, what will I do? I remembered that I had travelled to some furniture production companies in different parts of the world then as part of my backward integration plan. But I had laid aside the papers of my findings.

And with the new development, I knew what I needed to do at that point was to revisit my abandoned findings. Even though our cash-flow had now decreased with the ban, with the support and encouragement of my husband, families, pastors and friends I began my moves, travelling to different companies to discuss with them to come with us to Nigeria.

I looked at our whole product chain and discovered that the least competitive was the office seating. Even now we have few manufacturers of office seating globally as against desks and other furniture type. I had the privilege of being linked and working with one of the top ten office seating manufacturers as one of their own top ten dealers. So with a God-induced boldness, I went to SOKOA SA of France and discussed with them on the need to come to Nigeria with me. They laughed at first, because as a company which did not have any investment outside the shores of France at that time, Nigeria was the least attractive place they would have considered if they had wanted to start a foreign investment, considering all the things that have been said about us.

But I was undeterred. For two days we held series of meetings, and then I left. Few weeks later, they sent me a memorandum of understanding stating their intention to come into the venture with technical support and very little investment. I took it, knowing that God would do the rest. I continued working with my financial advisers, Frontier Capital, on the project. Later, SOKOA SA agreed to increase their investment in the Nigerian project to 21%. And with their full participation guaranteed, we had the confidence to approach the banks for their participation under the SMEIS scheme. Guaranty Trust Bank bought into the venture with a 32% shareholding, two of my friends hold 5% each, while I hold 37%.

It is important for me to state here that there are many dreams that never come to pass because of the tendency on the part of the dreamer to want to do it all alone. They are afraid that others might steal their ideas. The reality of the present day business is that it is more risky for one person to handle it all alone. There is a need to partner with others in strategic alliances. The key to this is that we must measure what our value system is compared to our prospective partners. Similarity of purpose and commitment to the same goals, both long and short-term, are essential consideration for partnership.

For SOKOA SA, the track record we had built over the years was a major factor in our favour when it got to a point of asking for their partnership. They have noted us for our integrity and were sure that we will not change overnight. GTB, on the other hand, has been my banker for a long time and that helped to justify their investment in us. So I advise all aspiring entrepreneurs to please build their financial records and maintain a good track record. You never know when you will need it.

Anyway, the story of Sokoa Chair Centre is now stale. The company has since been born on May 10, 2005. I am glad to say that our investors are not disappointed as we have started paying dividends from the second year. And the success story continues.

Since the opening of Sokoa Chair Centre, I have gone ahead to set up another company called

Furniture Manufacturers Mart. That is the arm of our business that is responsible for the production of wooden and laminate processing for my retail business and other furniture manufacturers. I realised at this point that the most important thing is not just building my own business alone, but helping to build the entire industry so that our country can stand tall, at least in the West African region.

Everyday I encounter many Nigerians, male and female, with skills in the sector, but who lack the resources and individual capacity to align with the skills they possess. Personally I believe the government is not in a position nor have the capacity to develop the segment. Where we have comparative advantage, a lot depend on all of us in the private sector to use what we have for the development of the country in a way that we can create jobs for our nephews, our nieces and many young men and women walking around looking for what to do in the midst of plenty.

Talking about retirement, it has been a joking matter for a while between my friends and I that I intend to retire at age 50, so as to have time for the social entrepreneurship projects which has always been in my heart to do. I have however been advised by a father-figure and someone whom I greatly respect that it is necessary to phase such projects over a period of time and not just drop off at work and get on the projects just like that. And I see a lot of wisdom in what he said.

My present obligation is to build each of the companies that God has used me to set up to a place of no return. I have a vision of making them globally competitive, structurally sound, and productively efficient and profitable, such that they can enter the stock market with celebrated prices and an agenda to outlive me.

I have no set agenda that it must be my children who should succeed me. I know God has helped me to do all that I did, and I will have to hand over to the next generation of competent people who can move it to the next level.

By the way, you will notice that at the beginning of my story I listed all the names I was given at my christening, and I am certain that you could not find Ibukun in the list. I forgot to tell the story.

One day, after I had given my life to Christ, the Lord spoke through a prophecy in church, announcing that my name would henceforth be called Blessing and went on to make certain pronouncements concerning that name. As someone who is so proudly Nigerian and does not like English names, I promptly translated the word blessing into Yoruba, and the answer is IBUKUN. So as often as you call me by that name you are helping heaven to declare God's heart over my life.

When I exit, I would like the following to be said about me and written on my epitaph:

"Here lies a life that was lived to the fullest and a body that died empty, having used all the talents that God gave me for His purpose and the benefits of humanity."

EPILOGUE
THE LEARNING POINTS

Reading through the stories of these women, one can see that a number of factors stand out which are common to all in the process of converting their dreams to a realistic enterprise.

Let's have a look at some of these factors and try to decode their relevance in the success of these women.

Dissatisfaction With The Status Quo
The first thing that is common to all the women whose stories were featured is that they all had a season of dissatisfaction with their lives or jobs at a point in time. They had become restless, bored or extremely dissatisfied with the status quo. They however did not feel helpless or unable to do anything about it. They all took responsibility for their lives by ACTING!

Even those who had plum jobs with good salaries and other perks of a good position got to points in their lives when the hitherto attractive golden handcuffs restraining their hands from venturing into something else became unattractive to them.

Kofo resigned from a management job in a bank to sit at home whilst trying to figure out what next.

Yewande "abandoned" a high profile, high paying job in a bank to go and bear "other people's burden" of organising parties and functions, or so it seemed to those who thought she was insane to make such a move.

For Kofo, Yewande, Ngozi or any of these women, they decided that the pursuit of their passion was worth every loss of the "big fat salary" and the risk of failure that was a possibility.

If you find yourself in a similar situation today, I am sure you would have learnt a few lessons and received some level of inspiration to take that step into the world of your passion to discover.

A wise man once said, "The best time to do anything is NOW! The second best time is Today!"

The Bible says "Now is the appointed time, today is the day of salvation" (2 Corinthians 6:2). So get on your feet and make that move. What is the worst thing that can happen? FAILURE? So what? You will not be the first or the last to fail. When you fail, you get up and TRY AGAIN and AGAIN until you get it right. This is what makes life fun!

Anyway, you will never know what is waiting for you until you try. Some of the greatest discoveries of all time were made through mistakes!

Aligning Business With Passion
The women whose stories are recounted in this book developed their businesses around their passion and interest; not on their whims or the rave of the moment.

This is a vital lesson for all would-be entrepreneurs. It is not enough to decide to go into business; it is advisable that you:

A. Pursue a business line in the areas of your passion and interest
B. Build a business to meet certain needs you have observed in the society which you possess the skills or training to meet

C.   Develop a business around a societal need that is not met to the satisfaction of the consumers, but which you know that you are able to deliver on beyond the expectation of the market

The mistake most entrepreneurs make is to start a business that is totally at variance with their passion and interest. Most of the time they settle for a line of business simply because it is perceived to be very lucrative, or is the reigning business in town. This is a mistake and it has contributed to the high number of businesses which do not exceed the first two years, as research has shown that 70-80% of new businesses do not survive beyond the first two years.

Every business will face a trying period or a series of challenges at some point in time. At such times, it is the entrepreneur's love and passion for what he/she is doing that will keep him/her going more than anything else. When everybody gives up, your passion, interest, skills and commitment will keep you going till you find the solution to the challenges.

SEARCH FOR INFORMATION AND DUE DILIGENCE

When one has identified one's area of passion or interest, it is important to gather all necessary information and knowledge pertaining to the field of interest.

Most of the women in this book have successfully built businesses in areas where they were not originally trained for. Oyinade, a trained lawyer makes some of the most beautiful wedding and other type accessories that I have ever seen anywhere in the world. The realisation that she had a natural talent in that area did not make her just jump into it and end up building a mediocre company that will go nowhere. She went away for two years in search of the skills and knowledge necessary to build such a business. That investment in knowledge and the continuous updating of herself are responsible for what she has done with Satin & Lace as a company.

The same applies to all these women as they invested time, energy and resources to develop themselves in the business areas they have chosen and I am certain that if you ask any of them they will tell you that it is a continuous process. Using myself as an example, I know I never stopped going to the Furniture Fairs abroad as a way of keeping up with developments in the industry. And I know that same is true for Ifeyinwa, Moni Fagbemi and Muni Shonibare.

In addition to the fairs, I joined the chief executive programme of Lagos Business School in 2000 and by 2003 was off to IESE Business School in Barcelona to join the Global Executive MBA class for the next 18 months. It was not because I had nothing better to do, but I was searching for knowledge and skills that will help me to continue to move the business forward. Without a doubt, every knowledge I gained added immeasurable value to where my business is today.

What all the above really means is that YOUR NATURAL TALENT, IDEAS, AND PASSION IS NOT ENOUGH! You need to seek for information and carry out due diligence of all that is involved in the business that you want to go into and continue to do the same even when running the business.

Apprenticeship
All of these women had some form of apprenticeship before they ventured out on their own. In other words, they had some working experience which afforded them the privilege of understanding the operations and internal structures of a corporate establishment, and what is required to set up a company.

I usually counsel most young people, who want to start their own business like yesterday, to go and get some working experience first, as the value of the exposure, the knowledge and the network they would be availed with in the process cannot be quantified. Even the Bible says that if you have not been faithful in what belongs to another, you will not be given what is yours (Luke 16:12). The season of working or service also teaches the discipline of the workplace, which will contribute in no small measure to the building of a successful enterprise.

The time of working also serves as a period when one can save towards the capital required to start your dream business. It is easier to ask people to help you, when they see your own sacrifice and commitment to that which you want to do.

Faith
As you read through the story of many of the "girl entrepreneurs", you cannot but feel they were preaching as they freely talked about their faith in God and the role God played in their business success.

There are many roles that our faith in God plays in our business life:

(a)   Our Value System
A woman's faith in God and commitment to her God will directly affect the things that she holds dear, and the rules by which she guides her life.

It is important at this point to separate a woman who lays claim to a faith solely because she was born into that faith from a woman who understands her faith and has made a conscious commitment to live by the values that are inherent in that faith.
Let us look at a woman who says that she is a Christian and whilst purporting to be a Christian feels very comfortable to pay a bribe, takes advantage of an undiscerning customer by over-

pricing, sells a fake product as real (including circumstances where the fake product like pharmaceuticals can result in a life and death situation), among many other vices of the market place of today.

A careful search through the Bible will provide scriptures that directly instruct against a Christian engaging in any of these actions. For example, consider what the Bible says on the following issues:

On Bribery
Proverbs 15:27:
He that is greedy of gain troubles his own house; but he that hates bribes shall live.

Proverbs 17:23
A wicked man accepts a bribe behind the back to pervert the ways of justice.

Proverbs 29:4
The king establishes the land by justice: but he who receives bribes overthrows it.

On Ill-Gotten Wealth
Proverbs 10:2:
Treasures of wickedness profit nothing: but righteousness delivers from death.

Proverbs 16:8:
Better is a little with righteousness than great revenues without justice.

Proverbs 28:8
One who increases his possessions by usury and extortion gathers it for him who will pity the poor.

Proverbs 20:21
An inheritance gained hastily at the beginning will not be blessed at the end.

Proverbs 13:11
Wealth gained by dishonesty shall be diminished: but he that gathers by labour shall increase.

Proverbs 28:20
A faithful man will abound with blessings: but he who hastens to be rich will not go unpunished.

Proverbs 28:22
A man with an evil eye hastens after riches, and does not consider that poverty will come upon him.

On Business Deception
Proverbs 11:1
A false balance is an abomination to the LORD, but a just weight is His delight.

Proverbs 21:6
Getting treasures by a lying tongue is the fleeting fantasy of those who seek death.

Proverbs 20:17
Bread gained by deceit is sweet to a man; but afterwards his mouth will be filled with gravel.

On Hoarding
Proverbs 11:26
He that withholds corn, the people shall curse him: but blessing shall be upon the head of him that sells it.

On Compromising
Proverbs 25:26
A righteous man who falters before the wicked is like a murky spring, and a polluted well.

On Your Personal/Corporate Image
Proverbs 22:1
A good name is to be chosen rather than great riches, loving favour rather than silver and gold.

On Your Personal Hygiene At Work
Proverbs 23:4:
Do not overwork to be rich: because of your own understanding, cease.

In the light of the above scriptures, it is obvious that a woman who is truly committed to her God and lives by her faith, as she rightly should, would strive at every point to allow those values that are inherent in her faith to have an overriding influence on the way she conducts her business.

The unfortunate thing is that while most of us hold our belief in God dear to us and are actively involved in doing our own thing for God, the business world that we operate in now has developed a whole new set of rules which does not honour God, nor respects the laws of the land. And we are continuously being told that we cannot succeed in business if we do not engage in these practices.

Helping a woman to steal from an institution that has entrusted her with the position is considered an opportunity rather than embezzlement and a breach of trust; a woman using her femininity as a tool for prosperity is considered street-wise rather than prostituting; Selling a product at two or three times what it is really worth thus taking advantage of the ignorance of the buyer is considered as being smart; and many other scenarios that one can point at.

(b) The God Factor

Another way the faith element plays a vital role in one's entrepreneurial pursuit is that it avails the entrepreneur the partnership of God. God is the only One Who knows the end of all things from the very beginning. And by entering an alliance with Him in any venture, you will be availing yourself of His omniscience, His help and guidance every step of the way, His encouragement and motivation when the chips are down, as well as His tutelage and direction on the course to take at every point in time.

Our knowledge is at best limited. Our projections are mere assumptions. Only God knows the exactitude of what will happen tomorrow or what our projections will turn out to be. That is why we really need Him to guide us to take the right business decisions which will turn out to increase our bottom line at the end of the day. The Bible says "trust in the LORD with all your heart, and do not lean on your own understanding. In all your ways, acknowledge Him and He will direct your path" (Proverbs 3:5-6).

Meanwhile, an alliance with God in your business can only be possible if you obey His precepts and run your business by His commands, and not by worldly standards or the popular way it is being done.

Spouse And Family Support

All the women sound quite alike in talking about the role of their spouses and family. Without mincing words, they acknowledged the irreplaceable role of their husbands as well as the love, encouragement and support of their families.

The reality is that, no matter where you go in the world, the husband has a measure of authority and control over the wife's life, not only her career or business. It therefore becomes very important that every woman who wants to succeed in all facets of her life, including her business, has to consider the following points:

a. If she is single, it is important to consider very carefully the type of man that she marries vis-à-vis the vision and ambition which she has for herself.

b. If she is already married she must walk in wisdom and understanding such that she will gain the support of her husband.

An unsettled home and an unsupportive husband are distractions which will delay, and in some cases, stop women from actualising their full potentials and dreams.

I know many women who are stuck at one level of business or the other. They are unable to move the business to the next level using available resources from financial institutions or bringing in investors solely because their husbands have said a categorical NO!

Many of us women are also guilty of bad management of our business success either through pride or shirking of our responsibilities as wives and mothers. This results in unsecured and non-trusting husbands, both of which we cannot afford as women in business.

What most of the women probably did not tell you in their stories is the amount of sacrifices they make daily on all sides in order to continue to enjoy the support, love and encouragement of their husbands and other family members. I can tell you categorically that every sacrifice is worth the joy of winning on all fronts as a wife, a mother and actualising your dreams as a woman.

Staying Power

As you read through each woman's story, you cannot miss their recounting some of the challenges they encountered in the course of starting up their businesses as well as along the path of growing it. Yet none of them talked about any point where they gave up on the business because of the challenges.

Most people think that you encounter the real challenges only at the beginning or in the early years of the business. This is however not true. The challenges vary as you move from one stage of the business to another. The issue of challenges is a function of our attitude to it.

You can look at it from the perspective of an opportunity, and therefore your mindset will be positive and solution-centred. Whilst, on the other hand, if you view it from the perspective of a problem, it could overwhelm you and end up burying you.

Some of your best and biggest opportunities for growth are embedded in your most trying moments. Think about it. Most problems you are likely to encounter will be common to other people in your own industry. If it is enough to overwhelm you, it has probably overwhelmed some of the other people as well. Now who do you think will emerge as the star of the pack? The one that gives up at the sight of the challenge or the one that stays long enough to solve the problem? I am certain of your answer. Only the person with the staying power to last the race will lead the pack!

The truth is many will give up along the path, but all these women have a story to tell only because they stayed in the race and I know they are still running. Watch out! It's not over until it is over!

Partnership
Another pertinent business issue is partnership. And our example in this regard is the stories of Ifeyinwa Ighodalo and Moni Fagbemi. We all know how problematic a partnership of any kind can be when money is involved, not to talk of a partnership of two women! And for these two women to have been in partnership for about 20 years and be successful at it is no mean achievement in the least! Their story is indeed an inspiration to so many women who might want to go into a joint venture.

Not that partnership is bad in itself. It is the way it is handled by the individuals involved, as well as the many preconceived prejudices against it, that makes it something everyone would like to avoid. Going into partnership is one good way for an entrepreneur to raise the needed funds to get her business on stream, from the dream level to the height of reality. If you have a viable business idea but do not have the required funds to float the business, you can always get someone who has the fund and you two can start a partnership based on your mutually agreed terms.

Another way that partnership is very useful in a business endeavour is that you can get to form a synergy and therefore draw on your partner's strengths, especially in the areas where you are not as endowed. A popular saying posits that "two heads are better than one", and there can be no greater advocacy for business partnership than this saying. Two or more people coming into a business venture together will make better decisions, achieve much more and that will ultimately affect their bottom line.

Design Options is one of the leading furniture concerns in this country today, and the success of the business is due to the commitment, the resourcefulness, and the steadfastness of Moni and Ifeyinwa. The individual values they brought to the table have ensured that the company is where it is today. Not that they don't have issues, as you must have read in their stories, but their commitment to their friendship and the company above all else is what has helped them surmount all challenges and kept them going.

Their story is indeed an inspiration for everyone desiring to go into partnership, especially the womenfolk.

Insufficient Funding
One of the most frequently given excuses for not starting a business or a dream is insufficient funding. Well, none of the women had a lot of money to start. Yet they started! Now it's a case of "See me now!"

The Bible teaches us not to despise the days of humble beginnings. Sadly, there are many dreams or business ideas that have never seen the light of day because of "funding".

It is great to want everything perfect on Day one, but we all do not have the opportunity, and even if we do, it will be wise to test the theory of our business plan in a small format, so the cost of wrong assumptions in our business plan will be less.

Every business idea you have has a "small beginning" version. This will help you to test the theory or hypothesis that is called your "business plan" or "business idea."

With the issue of start-up size settled, it is easier to look for the smaller amount that is required to start. Do you have any savings or assets that are convertible to cash to invest in your dream? It is always a good place to start before you go to husbands, fathers, uncles etc. If you cannot sacrifice for your own dream, why should anybody else?

As women, we have a lot of our capital in our wardrobes and around our necks. It is not a crime to be a woman by loving clothes and jewellery, but everything has a season. When we have done that which we need to do by giving the dream or business a life, then we will have the confidence to approach financial institutions, whether micro or macro and they will have to listen to us as we have done our bit.

Every woman in this book had to learn the discipline of financial management so that their businesses could grow from within itself. All the things they had to do without along the way, I am sure they can better afford now. There is definitely not a single one of them that will walk into any bank today and will not find help.

Time and discipline has a value. It might be tough at the beginning, but once you can get it started, it becomes easier as the business itself will generate income, the rest is up to you and how you choose to apply or use the money it generates.

Challenges of Infrastructure, Government Policies, NEPA, Staff Attitude etc.

Finally, you would have also read that all these women, without exception, mention the problem of lack of infrastructural facilities, inauspicious government policies, erratic power and water supply, getting the right staff with the right attitude etc as some of the challenges they have faced or are still facing in their businesses.

You should therefore take note that you may have to contend with some of these issues as well. But the interesting thing about it is that you know that some people have faced and worked around these same challenges to attain success in their businesses. So you have been sufficiently forewarned and should therefore be fore-armed before you launch out. Many people over the years have used these challenges as the excuse for not getting started at all. Whilst these problems are real, they are common to ALL other entrepreneurs in the Nigerian market, hence no one has an advantage over you in the local market.

When I started my business about 20 years ago, these problems were in existence. Almost 20 years later, they are still here! Imagine if I never got started, and if I am still waiting for a perfectly conducive environment to express myself. It will be impossible, if I were to start today, to find the same set of opportunities and develop the networ' which has been a part of the factors of my success.

Not to now talk of having the same energy which I had starting at the age of 25 as opposed to trying to start the same business under a perfect condition at age 45!

Timing is a major factor in business. When a business opportunity presents itself, for which you have the right sets of skills, a good intuition or leading in your spirit to go with, the issue of whether the environment is fully conducive becomes secondary. There will always be challenges, some of which will be fundamental and infrastructural, but those are the conditions that give birth to pioneers and provide the first mover's advantage to discerning would-be entrepreneurs. Remember Yewande's story. Event management, as a major business, was unheard of in Nigeria yet she gave up a major top management banking job to pursue what many considered a "foolish" dream. Only five years after, she has had the pleasure of opening the way for many businesses, providing jobs for hundreds of Nigerians to emerge in a sector that did not exist before she set up Eventful.

Ifeyinwa and Moni sensed, when they were starting, that there were enough people willing to pay for interior design services at that point, for them to leave their jobs and step out to set up Design Options. A perfectly conducive environment for an interior design company to function successfully will require many manufacturers of good quality furniture amongst various service providers needed for that business. None of which existed in any tangible or reliable form when they or Muni Shonibare were starting. They all worked with the limitations of what was available at the point in time and ended up integrating backwards to set up their own manufacturing facilities as a way forward to achieve their goals. Where there is a will, there will always be a way. Challenges in business only force your creative talents to reach deeper for solutions either by yourself or in collaboration or partnership with those around you.

In other words, there is no excuse for you to give up in the middle of, or not to succeed in your own entrepreneurial endeavor because you have been availed with the stories of like people who have braved all the peculiar odds of Nigerian female entrepreneurship and succeeded at it. If they could do it, you can do it as well. So go live your dream, build your enterprise and make Nigeria proud. Light a candle of bravery. So another young woman, or man for that matter, can see the way.

CPSIA information can be obtained
at www.ICGtesting.com
Printed in the USA
LVHW041642130621
690121LV00003B/637